THE ORIGINS OF
SIMULTANEOUS INTERPRETATION:
The Nuremberg Trial

Perspectives on Translation

The "Perspectives on Translation" series consists of works that analyse translation from a theoretical or practical point of view. In addition to the history, methodology, and theory, the series covers lexicology, terminology, interpretation... Textbooks for students as well as for professional translators and interpreters can be found in the "Didactics of Translation" series. Both series welcome manuscripts written in either English or French.

Didactics of Translation

Catering to the needs of students in schools of translation and interpretation, the textbooks published in this series are also very helpful to professional translators and interpreters who wish to improve their technique. The series' titles cover various fields in the discipline such as general translation and specialized translation as well as editing, writing, and lexicology for translators.

Advisory committee:

Jean Delisle, Series Director, University of Ottawa
Marie-Christine Aubin, Collège universitaire de Saint-Boniface
Annie Brisset, University of Ottawa
Luise von Flotow, University of Ottawa
Daniel Simeoni, McMaster University
Paul St Pierre, Université de Montréal
Lawrence Venuti, Temple University (Philadelphia)
Agnès Whitfield, York University

PERSPECTIVES ON TRANSLATION

THE ORIGINS OF SIMULTANEOUS INTERPRETATION:
The Nuremberg Trial

Francesca GAIBA

University of Ottawa Press
Ottawa

Canadian Cataloguing in Publication Data

Gaiba, Francesca

The Origins of Simultaneous Interpretation: The Nuremberg Trial

(Perspectives on Translation)
Includes bibliographical references.
ISBN 0-7766-0457-0

1. Court interpreting and translating – Germany – Nuremberg – History. 2. Nuremberg War Crime Trials, Nuremberg, Germany, 1946-1949. I. Title. II. Series.

JX5437.8.F73 1998   341.6′9   C98-900266-7

University of Ottawa Press gratefully acknowledges the support extended to its publishing programme by the Canada Council, the Department of Canadian Heritage, and the University of Ottawa.

Cover Design: Robert Dolbec

Cover Picture: *Interpreters at work*. From left to right: Capt. Macintosh, British Army, translates from French into English; Miss Margot Bortlin, translates from German into English. Source: National Archives, College Park, MD.

 UNIVERSITY OF OTTAWA
UNIVERSITÉ D'OTTAWA

ISBN-07766-0457-0

  542 King Edward, Ottawa (Ont.), Canada K1N 6N5
  press@uottawa.ca   http://www.uopress.uottawa.ca

Printed and bound in Canada

Next day Allied officers handed copies of the indictment to each of the defendants in the lightless cells of Nürnberg prison. Informed that they could choose their attorneys from prepared lists, the indicted reacted variously:...

Reich Marshal Hermann Göring: "Of course I want counsel. But it is even more important to have a good interpreter."

"Germany: The Defendants."
Time (29 Oct. 1945): 38

TABLE OF CONTENTS

HISTORICAL BACKGROUND

    The Nuremberg Trial: Historical Overview
    Interpretation before 1945
    The Invention of Simultaneous Interpretation
    Interpreting at the League of Nations in Geneva

PRETRIAL ARRANGEMENTS

    The Special Linguistic Needs of the Nuremberg Trial
    Bringing Simultaneous Interpretation to the Nuremberg Trial
    Supply and Installation of IBM Equipment
    Recruitment of the Interpreting Personnel
        Initial Recruiting at the Pentagon
        The Test at the Pentagon
        The Recruitment Process in Europe
        Testing and Hiring Interpreters in Nuremberg
        Criteria of Selection
        Results of Selection
        Training
        Dress Rehearsals
    The Translation Division

FOREWORD

The Nuremberg Trial against leading Nazi war criminals, conducted from November 1945 to August 1946, was one of the great and unique events of the twentieth century. The complete record of the trial in daily transcripts and supporting documents was published shortly thereafter in more than 40 volumes. Estimates vary, but it has been referred to as a "six-million-word trial." Yet, unbelievable as this may sound, not one word is said in this official, published record about the system of simultaneous interpretation that was created in order to permit the multilingual conduct of the trial.

This book is now setting the record straight. Generated by the imagination and curiosity of a young, multilingual student of history, it tells a remarkable story that has not been told before: How it came about that oral presentations made in one language can now be heard and understood in several other languages at the same time. For those of us who were there at the beginning, it has been hard to understand the complete lack of acknowledgement throughout these many years. It seems, however, that history will always get its due, thanks to young inquiring minds who take the time and trouble to collect, compile and present the evidence.

The system of simultaneous interpretation was crafted by trial and error in an attic room of the Nuremberg Palace of Justice. It served its purpose well and without it the trial would have taken four times as long. To some, at first, the very idea of multilingual instantaneous interpretation was unthinkable—as was the thought of bringing to trial the willing accomplices of a brutal dictator. By now, more than 50 years later, it is evident that simultaneous interpretation has been a success. It is used all over the world and has greatly improved communication, thereby promoting, it is hoped, a better understanding among nations. What remains to be seen is that the same acceptance and success be granted to the principles of justice and human rights that were promulgated by the Nuremberg Tribunal.

E. Peter Uiberall
Hollin Hills, February 1997

To my parents

ACKNOWLEDGEMENTS

I would like to thank the Nuremberg interpreters and Nuremberg staff that I contacted for providing me with precious material: Mr. Uiberall and Mr. Steer especially, and Ms. Coliver, Ms. Heyward, Mr. and Mrs. Horn, Mr. Horsky, Ms. Jordan, Mr. Ramler, Ms. Skuncke, Mr. Sprecher, Mr. Treidell and Ms. Patricia Vander Elst: without their help and patience in answering my questions, this book would not have been possible. I hope this work will render just testimony to their pioneering efforts and accomplishments in the interpreting profession. My thanks go to Professor Raffaella Baccolini, my thesis coordinator at the University of Bologna, to Professor Maria Rosa Bollettieri Bosinelli, Director of the School for Interpreters and Translators of Forlì, and to Gabriele Mack, Assistant Professor, and Peter Mead, lecturer at the School for Interpreters and Translators of Forlì, for their assistance and academic support. I am grateful to my advisor at the University of California at Berkeley, Professor Adamthwaite, for opposing my initial decision to give up the research, and to Professor Robert A. Rubinstein, Director of the PARC Program at Syracuse University, who helped and advised me during the publication of this book. I am also grateful to Mr. Jean Delisle and the staff of the University of Ottawa Press for believing that my manuscript was worth transforming into a book. Members of various institutions have also been friendly and helpful: Caroline Davis at the Syracuse University Special Collection Department; Margareta Bowen, Head of the Division of Interpretation and Translation of Georgetown University; Robert Godfrey of IBM Archives; the staff of the National Archives in Washington, D.C. and of the Public Records Office in London. Finally, I would like to thank the A. Schiavi Foundation of Forlì for their continuous contribution in funding this research and its publication. A special thank-you is of course devoted to my parents, to whom this work is dedicated, because they made all this possible.

GLOSSARY AND DEFINITIONS

I will define here the two most recurring words of this book, namely, "Nuremberg" and "interpretation." The War Crimes Trial of 1945-1946 in Nuremberg was not the only trial that the International Military Tribunal held. There were 12 so-called Subsequent Proceedings between 1946 and 1949. The Main and the Subsequent trials are generally referred to as the Nuremberg Trials. In this book, I refer to the first War Crimes Trial as the Nuremberg Trial, and I use the plural form only when what is being said refers to all the trials in general. Also, the adjective "Nuremberg" before a noun specifies the people and equipment of the Nuremberg Trial, for example, the Nuremberg interpreters. Finally, the spelling "Nuremberg" is an adaptation from the German *Nürnberg* and it is the one adopted in most French, American English and British English texts. According to Alfred Steer, Head of the Translation Division in Nuremberg, the Americans adopted it from the British, who imitated the French pronunciation.[1] The French add a third syllable, *-em-,* to the two-syllable German word, but they nasalize it strongly. English-speaking people do not nasalize and the result is a three-syllable word. Mr. Steer argues that the proper English name of the city should be "Nurnberg," a word that both American and British people can pronounce without difficulty. While agreeing with Mr. Steer that such a change in the spelling of *Nürnberg* is unnecessary, I feel that the spelling "Nuremberg" is settled in the English language. When consulting the library online catalogue, for example, the word to use is "Nuremberg"; no other spelling will access information. I therefore use the most common spelling for this word.

I would also like to briefly define the terms referring to interpretation that are used in this book. This may seem superfluous to those acquainted with this profession. But this work is addressed not only to professional interpreters. Its historical value, it is hoped, makes it interesting to scholars of other disciplines, who might not be familiar with these terms.

Translation.   Even though the terms "translation" and "interpretation" are often used interchangeably, they refer to two distinct, though related, activities or professions. Translators render the meaning of a written text into a different language, in written form. They read the text many times to understand it fully and become familiar with it, then translate it choosing the words that best express the ideas to be translated.

Interpretation.   Interpreters, on the other hand, work with the spoken language. They mediate the communication process on the spot between people speaking different languages. Interpreters hear the message in the source language, understand it and formulate the same message in the target language. Interpreters are required to be precise and accurate; however, the interpreting process is extemporaneous and interpreters cannot pause to pick the best words. They have to preserve tone, expression and choice of words of the speaker. There are different methods of interpretation that can be used, and they are selected according to their appropriateness to the proceedings:

Simultaneous interpretation with electric/electronic equipment. With this method, the information is transferred into the second language as soon as interpreters understand a "unit" of meaning. The word "simultaneous" is misleading, because interpreters have to understand a minimum of information before they can translate into the target language. The lag between the original and the interpreted version is called *décalage,* and its length varies according to the interpreters. It is usually no longer than seven or eight seconds. The speakers and the interpreters talk into microphones, the interpreters and the listeners wear earphones. With the simultaneous system, there is no need to pause after every sentence and wait for the translation or translations, as happens with consecutive interpretation. This is a great achievement in terms of saving time. Today this system is seldom used in courts because of its cost to the government.[2]

Simultaneous interpretation without equipment, also called *whispered interpreting*, or *chuchotage.*   It works in the same way as simultaneous interpretation, but there is no use of microphones and headphones. Interpreters sit next to the people who do not understand the working language and whisper the translation in their ears. In today's court cases, it is used mainly at the defendant's table for the use of the defendant.

Consecutive interpretation.   With this method, interpreters formulate the message in the target language *after* speakers have finished or given a portion of their speech. Speakers can also stop after every sentence to allow for interpretation. Interpreters take notes during the delivery of the original speech, using a particular technique of note-taking. Then they translate the speech by reading from their notes. This system is valid in terms of the accuracy of the translation, because it gives the interpreters the possibility to hear contextually relevant portions of the text before starting to translate. However, it is extremely inefficient in terms of time when numerous languages are involved. The duration of the event doubles with each additional language. Today it is the most common type of interpretation for witnesses at the witness stand and for cross-examination and briefings of witnesses. It is less expensive than simultaneous interpretation in terms of equipment and technical assistance, but by increasing the length of the proceedings it increases the overall cost of the trial.

Notes

1. Alfred G. Steer, letter to the author (April 7, 1995).
2. American Translators Association, "Court Interpreting and the Testing and Licensing of Interpreters." *ATA Chronicle* (October-November 1979): 7.

INTRODUCTION

The research for this book began as the answer to a simple question: "What is the origin of the profession of simultaneous interpretation?" Surprisingly, very little is known about the origins of the art and profession of simultaneous interpretation, which is now commonly used and even taken for granted at international conferences and gatherings. Of course, interpreters and translators have existed since the beginning of time, every time people speaking different languages have come in contact with each other. However, until less than a century ago, interpreting was not seen as a profession, and was performed by military officers, diplomats, secretaries or other personnel with knowledge of foreign languages. This changed with the creation of international organizations and the growing need of specialized linguistic personnel. This book focuses on one particular and specific aspect of the birth of the interpreting profession: the invention of simultaneous interpretation. Who, when and how, I wonder in this book, had the idea that it was possible to connect microphones and earphones in such a way that a speech could be translated *instantaneously* and *extempore* in a different language? Who thought it was possible for an interpreter to hear and speak at the same time?

This book answers these and other questions, and offers a complete overview of the birth of simultaneous interpretation by presenting a description of its workings at the 1945-1946 War Crimes Trial (Nuremberg, Germany). The Nuremberg Trial was the first official international gathering in which simultaneous interpretation was used. And this is what makes this topic fascinating. The research about the birth of simultaneous interpretation at the Nuremberg Trial is extremely interesting not only for the many professional interpreters and translators: it also adds a tile to the complex mosaic of our understanding and knowledge of the Main Nuremberg Trial, one of the most important events of twentieth-century history. Thus, the research about the origins of simultaneous interpretation does not only fill a gap in our knowledge about this profession but also covers new ground in the field of study about the Nuremberg Trial. Astonishing as it may seem, as Mr. Uiberall points out in the Foreword, the miracle of simultaneous interpretation did not receive any attention from historians. Thousands of volumes have been written about the trial, about its legal, political, historical aspects—but if we were to add all the parts dealing with the interpreting system, they would amount to about a dozen pages. In these books, interpreters receive as much attention as court stenographers, police officers or press correspondents. And yet, one thing should become clear by reading this book: the Nuremberg Trial would not have been possible without simultaneous interpretation.

When I first heard that the Nuremberg Trial was the birthplace of simultaneous interpretation, this spurred my curiosity because I know how difficult simultaneous interpretation is, and what long training and education it requires, and thus I wondered whether the use of untrained interpreters had an impact on the fairness of the trial. I decided to embark on this research project with the goal of finding a major mistake in the translation that changed the course of history. However, the scope and "hubris" of my plan diminished as I began the research and discovered that, before looking for mistakes in the material, I had first to find the material. This became the real challenge.

Published material about Nuremberg interpretation is extremely scarce. Only articles and generic references in history books have sporadically been written. Most of the sources of this book are unpublished. Some of them are available at institutions such as the National Archives in Washington, D.C. and the Public Records Office in London. Some other unpublished sources are available only to the author, since they are texts and letters that Nuremberg interpreters sent to me personally. Because of the paucity of sources, this book is not argumentative but descriptive: I am not defending a claim about the Nuremberg Trial; I am presenting all the information about simultaneous interpretation at Nuremberg that I could collect. I will therefore refrain from comments pertaining to the fairness of the trial or to similar controversial issues. The opinions, judgements and recollections of facts contained in the book are mainly those of the participants in the trial. The main strength of this book is the amount of information it provides, and the novelty of such a text among the literature of this field. This is the first text to give a complete overview of the simultaneous interpreting system at the Nuremberg Trial.

The focus of this work is solely the simultaneous interpreting system and simultaneous interpreters of the first, main War Crimes Trial. I will not deal with the so-called Subsequent Proceedings, where only two languages, German and English, were used, and I will not discuss the organization of the Translating Branch and their difficulties in keeping up with the enormous amount of work they were required to do.

The Research

My bibliographical research started in the *Universitätsbibliothek* (University Library) in Heidelberg, Germany; it was then carried out and completed at the libraries of the University of California at Berkeley and at various libraries in the United States. Since the beginning, the research has been carried out in two directions: history books about the Nuremberg Trials,[1] and texts about the history of interpreting and translating. The second search proved more fruitful at the University of Heidelberg, whose *Institut für Übersetzen und Dolmetschen* (Institute for Interpreters and Translators) has a small but specialized library, while the search of history books was carried out mainly at the University of California at Berkeley. There I found three copies of the original transcripts of the proceedings, 42 volumes each, and a rich selection of history books on the Nuremberg Trial, which, however, only occasionally devote a few paragraphs to the description of the interpreting system. The library also possesses microfiches of the 1945-1946 issues of the most important newspapers, and I searched for material in *The Times, The New York Times* and *Newsweek,* where I found a few specific articles, which provided the names of some interpreters and anecdotes about daily life in the courtroom.

A considerable part of the research was carried out through correspondence: I wrote to Syracuse University to get copies of the unpublished Francis Biddle Papers;[2] the National Archives in Washington, D.C. were able to provide copies of the Jackson Papers.[3] The Public Records Office in London was helpful in the search of documents of the British Prosecution. I wrote to every major translators' and interpreters' association in Europe and the United States; I wrote to universities where I knew Nuremberg interpreters had taught. The search was successful: after two months I was in touch with three Nuremberg interpreters, Peter Uiberall, Siegfried Ramler and Alfred Steer, who in turn gave me the names and addresses of other still living interpreters. They answered my numerous questions about the material I had found, which was often unclear or contradictory. They provided useful documents and recollections about the Nuremberg Trial. I later contacted other interpreters: Elisabeth Heyward, Edith Coliver, Frederick Treidell, Marie-France Skuncke, Patricia Vander Elst and Stefan Horn.

The AIIC office (International Association of Conference Interpreters) in Geneva, Switzerland sent me a copy of their videotape about Nuremberg interpretation. It contains interviews with Nuremberg interpreters and excerpts from the original motion picture of the trial. I later found out that besides London and Washington, there is unpublished material about the Nuremberg Trial also at the *Bundesarchiv* in Koblenz, Germany and in the Russian War Archives in Moscow. The material in Moscow has become accessible only now, and it has not as yet been fully explored. This might be an interesting possibility for a scholar with knowledge of Russian to continue and develop the research about interpretation and the Nuremberg Trial.

What is fascinating about the material I consulted for this research is its diversity. I did not just consult books. I received copies of manuscripts and typescripts, personal letters and telephone calls. I saw pictures, videotapes, microfilms, microreels. My knowledge of three of the four languages of the tribunal (I do not speak Russian) put me in an especially favorable position. Any book or material I found in French, German, Italian or English could be added to my working bibliography without problems of language.

I sometimes encountered the problem that sources, even primary ones, contradict each other. Peter Uiberall, interpreter and monitor at the trial, has given me an explanation of why even Nuremberg interpreters report different versions of the same event.

> The problem with "sources," especially 50 years after the facts, is that so many are not only secondary but also merely repeating hearsay or material from other secondary sources. And even with primary sources the key is whether the person had direct access to the information or merely heard about it later from others.[4]

Other interpreters report that sometimes Nuremberg episodes described in books in fact never happened, or maybe they first originated on the basis of an actual event, but changed through the course of 50 years because of hearsay and repetitions. Being in direct contact with the interpreters who worked at the Nuremberg Trial personally allowed me to check and cross-check the accuracy of reported events with the astonishing memory of many of the Nuremberg interpreters.

Notes

1. For an explanation of the usage of this term, see Glossary and Definitions.
2. Francis Biddle was the American judge of the bench.
3. Robert H. Jackson was the Chief Prosecutor of the American delegation.
4. E. Peter Uiberall, letter to the author (April 27, 1995).

CHAPTER ONE

BEFORE THE TRIAL

On November 20, 1945, Judge Lawrence opened the War Crimes Trial, the most important trial of the century. The eyes of the world, pointed on the crowded Nuremberg courtroom, for the first time in history marveled at something unknown: simultaneous interpretation, a technique that would allow communication among people speaking four different languages. But what made it possible for interpretation to be carried out in the first place? This chapter explores the path leading to the invention of simultaneous interpretation, the decision to use it and its installation in the courtroom. It provides a brief historical description of the Nuremberg Trial[1] and an overview of the interpreting profession before 1945. The historical introduction to the Nuremberg Trial is meant as a general overview of the most important facts of the event. Any juridical, historical or political assessment has purposely been withheld. The overview of pre-1945 interpretation shows the novelty and importance of the invention of the new method of simultaneous interpretation, which contrast with, and at the same time justify, the reluctance and hostility that many at the time showed against its introduction at Nuremberg.

HISTORICAL BACKGROUND

The Nuremberg Trial: Historical Overview

In view of the unparalleled atrocities committed by the Axis powers, especially by Germany, throughout the Second World War, numerous warnings were issued by the Allied powers that the perpetrators would be held responsible for their crimes before a court of law. In October 1943 the representatives of the 17 Allied nations except the U.S.S.R. met in London and established the United Nations War Crimes Commission (UNWCC). They laid down the general rules for the incrimination and prosecution of war criminals. Based on these rules the representatives of the major Allied powers, Great Britain, the U.S.S.R., the U.S.A. and the provisional government of France, signed the London Agreement on August 8, 1945. This agreement included the charter establishing an International Military Tribunal, whose task was the indictment and trial of major Axis power criminals. The agreement was accepted and signed by 19 other countries. The Charter listed the categories of crimes that would fall under its jurisdiction, namely, crimes against peace, crimes against humanity and conventional war crimes. Fairness to the defendants during the whole proceedings was given top priority. The defendants were entitled to receive a copy of the indictment at a reasonable time before the trial, with the possibility to give explanations to the charges against them. They were granted the right to have preliminary hearings and the proceedings conducted in or translated into their language. They were given the choice to defend themselves or to be represented by counsel. Finally, they would be allowed to cross-examine prosecution witnesses and introduce evidence for their defense.

The first official session of the tribunal was held in Berlin, on October 18, 1945 and was presided over by the Soviet member, General I.T. Nikitchenko. Only the judges took part in this closed session. Each of the original signatory countries sent a member and an alternate: Sir Geoffrey Lawrence sat for Great Britain, Donnedieu de Vabres for France and Francis Biddle for the U.S.A. They drafted the indictment against the top 24 Nazi criminals held prisoners by the Allies, charging them with numerous war crimes as defined by the UNWCC. The defendants included Hermann Göring, Rudolf Hess, Joachim von Ribbentrop, and other leading personalities of the German Reich.[2]

The actual trial took place in Nuremberg, starting November 20, 1945, under the presidency of Sir Geoffrey Lawrence (see Fig. I). The city of Nuremberg was chosen for several reasons. First, it had been the seat of major Nazi rallies. Moreover, it was under American occupation, and the United States was the only country at the time that could supply the wherewithal for the trial. The Chief Prosecutors at the trial were General R.A. Rudenko for the Soviet Union, François de Menthon and Auguste Champetier de Ribes for France, Sir Hartley Shawcross and Sir David Maxwell-Fyfe for the United Kingdom and

Justice Robert H. Jackson for the United States. Before the trial, one of the defendants, Robert Ley, committed suicide in his prison cell, while the industrialist Gustav Krupp was considered unable to stand trial because of his age and health condition.

The trial lasted more than 10 months, a total of 216 trial days, and reached its conclusion on October 1, 1946, when the judgement of the tribunal on the 22 defendants was read. Twelve defendants (including Martin Bormann tried *in absentia*) were sentenced to death by hanging, three were sentenced to life imprisonment, four received sentences between 10 and 20 years and three were acquitted.[3] The reading of the sentences was followed by a speech by General Nikitchenko, the Russian judge, expressing the Soviet dissent from the acquittals of the three defendants and the life imprisonment of Hess instead of his death sentence. Hermann Göring escaped his sentence by committing suicide in his cell. Despite the strict surveillance under which the defendants were kept, he managed to swallow a cyanide capsule and died the night before the sentences were carried out.

Subsequently, 185 other German personalities—cabinet ministers, industrialists, ambassadors, admirals and field marshals, jurists, physicians and so on—were brought to court before 12 tribunals composed solely of American judges. These Subsequent Proceedings, as they became known, were held in Nuremberg between December 1946 and March 1949, and were conducted in German and English only.

There is much disagreement about the trial, concerning its *raison d'être*, its fairness, its being or not "victors' justice." On one thing, however, there is consensus: the trial would not have been possible without the simultaneous interpretation into four languages. The mass media both praised and criticized it, but to insiders of the translating profession it was clear how revolutionary it was in the field. In order to appreciate the magnitude of its impact, it is necessary to take a step backwards into the history of interpretation.

Interpretation before 1945

Interpreting today is taken for granted at international conferences. There are permanent booth installations in every major conference hall around the world. It is, however, a remarkably new profession, whose origins date back to less than a century ago. Interpreting was born around 1920, after languages other than French were recognized as official diplomatic languages. Consecutive and whispering interpreting were the first techniques used;[4] interpreting at the League of Nations in

Geneva before the Second World War was similar to simultaneous interpreting, but simultaneous interpreting as we know it today was invented later, as explained in this chapter.

The need for interpretation at international conferences only developed during the First World War. Before that time French was the only official diplomatic language. At the Congress of Vienna in 1814-1815, for example, the participants were either diplomats with a perfect knowledge of French, or high ranking officers who had been selected expressly because they knew French. This was also the case at the meetings of the World Postal Union.[5] Moreover, communication between institutions speaking different languages was carried out mainly through dispatches and notes, which only required written translations.

During the First World War, however, some of the negotiators from the United States and Great Britain were not conversant with French, and this created the need for interpretation. Thus, at international meetings one of the diplomats would usually translate sentence by sentence for those who did not understand the working language. This was the first type of consecutive interpretation, and it was used, for example, during the sessions of the Armistice Commissions, which were held in French, English and German.[6] During these sessions, sentence-by-sentence interpretation was usually done by army interpreters or liaison officers.

Afterwards, during the preliminaries of the Paris Peace Conference, the British insisted on the recognition of English as an official diplomatic language. Every diplomatic matter therefore could, from then on, be discussed in French or in English, thus creating a permanent need for oral translation.[7]

The need for interpretation became more acute with the foundation of the League of Nations and the meetings of the International Labor Organization. At these meetings, the discussions dealt not only with diplomatic matters, but also with issues that did not normally appear on the agenda of international conferences, such as economic issues of recovery or labor issues. Inclusion of specific technical subjects in such discussions increased the need for expert linguists to carry out the translations. Moreover, it sometimes happened that groups of delegates, such as trade unionists, would speak neither English nor French. They were therefore supplied with interpreters who whispered them the translation of the proceedings in their languages and interpreted their speeches consecutively.

The increased need for qualified professional interpreters brought about the birth of the first School for Interpreters in Geneva in 1941. At that time the school trained the candidates in whispering and consecutive interpreting, and taught only four languages.[8] It was the only School for Interpreters in the world and was created to train professional interpreters mainly for the League of Nations in Geneva.[9]

In 1945, the Allies plus China met to lay down the Charter of the United Nations. At the San Francisco Conference in June 1945, and at the London meetings in early 1946, during which the first Secretary General was selected, interpretation was only consecutive, performed by famous interpreters, such as Jean Meyer, George Rabinotwitch and the Kaminker brothers, under the supervision of Jean Herbert. André Kaminker, together with his brother George, was the star of consecutive interpreting at the time, and could translate a one-and-a-half-hour speech without notes.[10]

Neither whispering nor consecutive interpreting were satisfactory methods of translation. Although whispered, the interpreter's voice interfered with the voice of the speaker. Moreover, only a small group of delegates could listen to the translation. As for consecutive, it was appallingly slow, because every sentence had to be repeated in every other working language. "Sessions were delayed interminably while translators slogged along well in the wake of the proceedings."[11] In addition, the majority of the delegates, after listening to the translation into their language, had to sit and wait for the action to proceed, while hearing languages they did not understand. International conferences needed a more efficient method, and the system of simultaneous interpretation was invented.

The Invention of Simultaneous Interpretation

Simultaneous interpretation was devised as an improvement of the consecutive and whispering modes. With simultaneous translation, the interpreter would give a running translation, that is, translate the text while hearing it. Thus, it would be less time-consuming than translating consecutively: a multilanguage conference could be carried out at the same speed as a one-language conference. Simultaneous interpretation was also more effective than whispering: interpreters would sit in soundproof booths and would not disturb the speaker. Their translation would be carried to all the participants at the conference through earphones.

Simultaneous interpretation was invented to work like this: through a system of electrical transmission, communication occurs through a wired system of microphones and headphones. Interpreters hear the original speech through headphones and translate it into the language to which they are assigned. By means of a selector switch, listeners can choose one of the various language channels, in order to hear either the original speech or the interpreted version of their preference.

The invention of the simultaneous interpretation system is described by André Kaminker, one of the first simultaneous interpreters in history, in a lecture given at the University of Geneva in 1955. Kaminker was one of the few interpreters working between the two world wars, and translated simultaneously Hitler's speech in 1934 for the French radio.[12] Kaminker was also interpreter at the League of Nations and later at the UN.[13] In the lecture he attributes the invention of simultaneous interpreting to Mr. Finlay and Mr. E.A. Filene, the latter a Boston businessman and member of the International Chamber of Commerce.

> [L'interprétation simultanée] ce n'est pas là une chose tout à fait nouvelle, cela date d'il y a longtemps déjà. C'est vers 1926 ou 1927 qu'un homme qui s'appelait Filene... d'accord avec un ingénieur électricien, M. Finley [sic], a inventé, ou a eu l'idée qu'il devait être sans doute possible d'écouter d'une oreille et de traduire en même temps dans une autre langue. Il s'en est ouvert à Thomas Watson qui est le président, encore aujourd'hui, de la "International Business Machines Corporation."
>
> D'accord à eux trois, ils ont pris un brevet—je me demande encore comment le brevet a été accordé, parce qu'il n'y a rien dans ce brevet. Il n'y a rien qui soit une invention quelconque, parce que le fait de mettre un micro avec trois ou quatre lignes et des plots qui passent de l'une à l'autre, ne peut être considéré comme une invention.[14]

The Filene-Finlay equipment was manufactured by IBM and used at the League of Nations fairly successfully. In a letter by IBM of 1945, it is stated that their International Translator System was being used at the League of Nations Headquarters in Geneva, and that this was the only permanent installation. It had also been used at other conferences such as the International Chamber of Commerce Convention in 1920 and the Fourth Pan-American Union Conference in Washington, D.C. around 1922.[15] These dates seem to contradict André Kaminker's claim that the system was invented in 1926 or 1927.

However, other sources confirm Kaminker's date. *L'Interprète* of 1946 reports that Filene had become increasingly dissatisfied with the language situation at the International Labor Organization meeting, in which he participated as one of the employers' representatives. He suggested that a "telephone translation" system be adopted.[16] The system that he invented together with Finlay and Thomas Watson became known as the IBM Hushaphone Filene-Findlay [sic] system, patented in 1926.[17] The Hushaphone was used for the first time on June 4, 1927 at a session of the International Labor Conference in Geneva, and reportedly saved the ILO £32,700.[18] Similar equipment, supplied by Siemens & Halske, was employed at the 1930 International Conference on Energy.[19]

Other sources mark the 15th International Congress of Physiology of 1935 in Leningrad as the first setting in which simultaneous interpretation was used. This conference was presided over by Pavlov and featured a wired translation system for five languages.[20] Pavlov's introductory statement was reportedly translated simultaneously into English, French and German.[21] Participants were given instructions on how to use the headphones and microphones.[22]

Interpreting at the League of Nations in Geneva

However, in Geneva and other international conferences before the war, interpreters did not actually perform simultaneous interpreting as it was later done at Nuremberg and as we know it today.[23] Admittedly, they were using the equipment devised for simultaneous interpreting, but they utilized it with different methods, which I will call "simultaneous successive interpretation" and the "simultaneous reading of pretranslated texts." With "simultaneous successive interpretation," the interpretations were simultaneous with each other, but not with the original speech. There was always at least *one* successive interpretation. At the League of Nations and the ILO, for example, the various interpreters would take notes on the original speech, as for the consecutive interpretation; after the end of the speech, one of the interpreters, usually the French interpreter, would take the stand and translate consecutively into his language. At the same time, the other interpreters, sitting in the booths and speaking into their microphones, gave their version of the speech in English, Spanish, etc., reading from their notes. In this way, the translation was still consecutive and therefore fairly accurate, and the time required to translate into all languages greatly reduced, in comparison to the normal consecutive mode. This system proved very useful at the League of Nations, but it still involved one successive interpretation, thus making the proceedings twice as long.[24]

In Geneva, the Filene-Finlay system was also used for the "simultaneous reading of pretranslated texts." This of course was only possible when the speakers were reading from texts that they had made available to the interpreters well in advance. The interpreters would translate the speeches before the session and read them at the same time as the original speech. With this system the proceedings were carried out as fast as in a conference involving only one language.

These two methods, "simultaneous successive interpretation" and the "simultaneous reading of pretranslated texts," both employed the Filene-Finlay equipment, but not for simultaneous interpreting as we know it today. This is why it is true that, as most texts say,[25] the *system* was not new and had already been used before Nuremberg, while "the *art* of simultaneous translation was virtually unknown at the time."[26]

"Simultaneous successive interpretation" and the "reading of pretranslated texts" were used fairly successfully at the League of Nations. However, the upcoming War Crimes Trial promised to be such an extraordinary event that it would require equally extraordinary language services.

PRETRIAL ARRANGEMENTS

The fact that the Nuremberg Trial would require special linguistic services was evident to all those who worked on its organization. The linguist Léon Dostert had the vision that extempore simultaneous translation would be the solution, but the decision to use it at the trial was hard to take because no delegation felt comfortable with the multilingual character of the trial and most believed at first that simultaneous interpretation would not work at all. Problems did not end once the decision was finally taken: installation presented some problems and recruiting was definitely the hardest task of all, given the novelty and difficulty of the job.

The Special Linguistic Needs of the Nuremberg Trial

Two constraints created linguistic obstacles at the trial and they are listed in the Charter of the International Military Tribunal. First, the charter ruled that the defendants had the right to a fair trial (Chapters IV and V), one prerequisite for this being that all the proceedings be translated into a language that the defendants understood, in this case German (Articles 16 and 25 respectively).[27] The use of traditional consecutive translation to meet this requirement would have meant that twice as much time—at least—would be needed for the trial. But the charter also ruled that the trial had to be carried out as expeditiously as possible, in order to reduce costs and time, and to keep the attention of the public and the media.[28]

A solution that would meet both requirements was to use only one working language, in this case, German. As mentioned earlier, this was common practice in international gatherings before the First World War, where participants spoke a common language, usually French. But the Nuremberg Trial differed considerably from diplomatic meetings. No one could have asked the whole International Military Tribunal to speak and understand German. First of all, discussions did not focus on one single topic: subjects ranged from foreign policy to sanitary conditions in concentration camps. The complexity of the issues at the trial was such that the prosecution could not be expected to carry out their work in a foreign language. Even if a British lawyer had sufficient knowledge of German legal terminology, he would have had a hard time in the description of the destruction of the Warsaw ghetto, for example. Moreover, a fair trial was to be granted to the defendants, a trial in which they had the right to speak and hear their own language so that they would meet no obstacle to the exercise of their rights. The same fairness had to be granted to the English, French, Russian and American prosecutors and judges. Finally, the Nuremberg Trial was one of the first major international media events, and there was the need to keep the international public constantly informed. For these reasons, the tribunal could not limit itself to one working language. It was thus decided that every Allied nation involved would have the right to use its own language.

Moreover, the Nuremberg Trial needed a new type of interpretation because of its difference from other interpreted trials. Usually, when a witness or a defendant speaks a language different than that of the tribunal, a sworn interpreter is hired to sit next to the person and whisper the translation in his or her ear. When the witness or the defendant speaks, the interpreter translates simultaneously or consecutively into the microphone. This is a method still used today, but it only works if there is just one person who does not speak the language of the tribunal; the linguistic interference with the proceedings is minimal, even if there is a small delay. But at Nuremberg the working languages were four, and not only one person, but whole groups of people spoke different languages. Furthermore, the language service at interpreted trials is usually for the sole communication between the witness or defendant and the rest of the tribunal. At the IMT trial language barriers existed among the very members of the bench, and among the various teams of prosecutors, who needed to interact in order to carry out a consistent prosecution.[29]

Because of these special linguistic features of the Nuremberg Trial, the organizers realized that traditional interpreting methods would not be applicable to the IMT trial. Traditional consecutive and "simultaneous successive interpreting" would increase the length of the trial by four and two times respectively, while the charter asked for a quick trial. The simultaneous reading of pretranslated texts would require participants to write their speeches in advance. Obviously, this was not feasible in a trial, where participants talk extempore, especially during examination and cross-examination.

Moreover, the members of the court feared the failure of traditional interpreting methods; they already had first-hand experience of them. Language problems had surfaced already at the London talks where the charter was being discussed. Also the minutes of the October 29, 1945 meeting of the judges in Berlin contain numerous remarks about linguistic difficulties. Members often complained that they could not hear the English translation of French remarks and on some occasions the French-into-English translation was made by Judge Biddle himself.[30] The language confusion at those small meetings gave the principals the idea of how appalling the trial would be, if the language problem would not be solved. They were also well aware of "the difficulties experienced by the British in the Belsen trials which involved only two languages (English and German) and yet which bogged down because of the interpreting problem."[31] A quote by Justice Jackson, the U.S. prosecutor, is revealing of the then prevailing mood about the language situation:

> I think that there is no problem that has given me as much trouble and as much discouragement as this problem of trying to conduct a trial in four languages. I think it has the greatest danger from the point of view of the impression this trial will make upon the public. Unless this problem is solved, the trial will be such a confusion of tongues that it will be ridiculous, and I fear ridicule much more than hate.[32]

In conclusion, at Nuremberg, consecutive interpretation, the reading of pretranslated texts and "simultaneous successive interpreting" would not have proved feasible. A new system had to be found that would allow a fair trial to be carried out quickly—something that had never been performed before at such a crucial event as the IMT trial. Someone in Washington, D.C. was already thinking about the solution: extempore simultaneous interpretation.

Bringing Simultaneous Interpretation to the Nuremberg Trial

Who was the person that first thought of extempore simultaneous interpreting as the optimal solution to Nuremberg linguistic problems? There appears to be controversy among the sources, which indicate alternately Justice Jackson, the U.S. Chief Prosecutor, and Léon Dostert, later Chief of the Translation Division at Nuremberg.

Most Nuremberg historians, like Conot and Kahn, tend to attribute the "discovery" of the interpreting system to Justice Jackson. They say that he brought the simultaneous system from Geneva to Nuremberg. These authors do not mention Colonel Léon Dostert nor credit him with having introduced the simultaneous system to Nuremberg; if they mention him, they do so only in regard to the recruitment of personnel, because he was the Head of the Translation Division at the beginning of the trial. However, more specific texts about the Nuremberg Trial reveal the involvement of Colonel Dostert in the introduction of simultaneous system to Nuremberg to its full extent, as do texts written by Dostert himself and by Nuremberg interpreters. Some interpreters (Ramler) I wrote to asking for clarification did not even know of any involvement of Jackson's in the matter, and are convinced that Dostert was the person who brought the simultaneous system to Nuremberg.

There is a reason for this discrepancy.[33] During the pretrial stage, in the summer of 1945, Dostert was "working" from Washington, while Jackson was in Europe arranging for the trial and meeting other prosecutors. Those who were in Europe were under the impression that Jackson himself had the idea of simultaneous interpreting, while in fact he received instructions or suggestions from Washington. Interpreters like Peter Uiberall who were recruited by Dostert at the Pentagon in Washington saw the process from a different angle, and came to know about Dostert's efforts in promoting the simultaneous system in Nuremberg.

Colonel Léon Dostert, who had been Eisenhower's interpreter during the war and had his office at the Pentagon, was responsible for language services in foreign affairs. Being an interpreter and a professional linguist at Georgetown University, he knew about the Filene-Finlay system used at the League of Nations and at other international conferences.[34] He also knew that the way they were using the system there was unsatisfactory. "It was Dostert who was convinced that the existing apparatus, with some modification, could be used for *spontaneous, immediate* interpretation."[35] This was the revolutionary idea in the field of interpretation. He most probably heard of Jackson's concerns about the linguistic problems of the Nuremberg Trial at the Pentagon, and thought that the Filene-Finlay system could be adapted to suit the needs of the trial. He contacted Mr. Suro, Chief Translator of the State Department, and informed him of his idea.[36] He also contacted Charles H. Horsky, who was "in charge of the Washington headquarters of Justice Jackson's operation as Nuremberg prosecutor."[37] Dostert explained to Horsky how the interpreting system would work and convinced him that it was the best solution for the Nuremberg Trial.

In the meantime in Europe Jackson had sent his son William to the League of Nations in Geneva to see how the linguistic problem had been solved there. William Jackson reported that their system of consecutive translation was appallingly slow. At this point, Horsky from Washington, D.C. cabled Justice Jackson, who was in London arranging for the trial with other prosecutors, and told him not to make any arrangements for the language services because an instantaneous system of interpretation could be used. As reported in the minutes of the meeting of the Chief Prosecutors in London on August 31, 1945:

> Mr. Jackson reported that he had received a suggestion from America for the installation of a system of multiple and simultaneous translation. It was considered possible that such a system would be capable of adaptation for the purpose of the trial.[38]

After receiving this advice, Justice Robert Jackson sent his son and Brigadier General Gill, his executive, to Washington to take a look at the equipment. Here they met Charles Horsky. Dostert, in the meantime, had perfected the system and even trained a few interpreters for the demonstration, to which he invited Charles Horsky and William Jackson:

> In an auditorium at the Pentagon, Horsky and young Jackson were met by a short, dapper army colonel with a pronounced French accent... Dostert asked Horsky and Ensign Jackson to have a seat midway back in the auditorium and proceeded to place earphones on their heads. On the stage were three men and a woman, each with a separate microphone. Off to one side, an IBM engineer stood before a control panel.

> Dostert called out to the woman on the stage, who began to speak extemporaneously in English... The three men began speaking into their microphones in a babel of tongues... What they were getting, Dostert explained, was everything the young woman had been saying in English translated, almost as she spoke, into the three other languages that would be used in the trial.[39]

William Jackson and Horsky found that the system was suited for the Nuremberg Trial, and cabled Justice Jackson in Nuremberg to report to him. On September 5, 1945 Horsky met with Suro, the Chief Translator of the State Department to discuss the use of the equipment that Dostert had shown. He then wrote again to Justice Jackson to explain the functioning of the equipment in detail.[40]

Dostert managed to convince Jackson and his staff that the system was suited for the trial, but the same task turned out to be difficult for Jackson's staff, when they explained the workings of the system to the delegations of France, the Soviet Union and Great Britain. The reaction of prosecutors and judges swung between simple concern and overt skepticism. It was for them hardly credible that one single system could provide access to four languages simultaneously. Moreover, it seemed to them a task beyond human capabilities to hear and speak at the same time in different languages. They felt uncomfortable about the way it would work, and they doubted it could provide a reliable record of the proceedings. Specifically, the Chief Prosecutors expressed doubt that the system might function for witness examination; they believed it would only work when reading pretranslated versions of defense and prosecution prepared speeches.[41]

Even Justice Jackson was skeptical about it. He agreed to have the equipment shipped to Nuremberg but was not fully convinced that it would work. He even proposed to the tribunal to use as few witnesses as possible and to introduce written documentary evidence instead, in order to minimize the use of interpretation of oral testimony.[42] However, he knew that the alternatives to simultaneous interpreting were worse, and he was ready to try the system before forming a judgement.

Others were skeptical about simultaneous interpreting for different reasons. André Kaminker, for instance, Interpreter in Chief of the French delegation, who had been experimenting with simultaneous interpretation between the two world wars, thought that simultaneous interpretation would not be feasible at Nuremberg because it was not possible for the speakers to check the accuracy of the interpretation. In such highly critical proceedings, he claimed, the defendants and speakers in general would need to be sure that the translations of their testimony were accurate. Simultaneous translation does not allow this; after the trial, Kaminker thus justified his skepticism:

> Lorsque le procès de Nuremberg est venu, procès qui, s'il m'était permis de le dire, semblait théoriquement, humainement tout au moins, être le dernier endroit où l'on pouvait introduire l'interprétation simultanée, parce que les hommes jouaient leur tête, et qu'il était impossible pour eux de suivre et de contrôler—ce qui est évidemment le gros reproche qu'on peut faire à la simultanée—on l'a introduite tout de même.[43]

In October 1945, two months after Jackson had started campaigning for simultaneous interpreting, the other delegations still had reservations about it. They were still uncomfortable with the idea of simultaneous interpreting and preferred old methods. At the IMT meeting of October 29, 1945, the French delegation put forward a proposal that had been formulated by their Interpreter in Chief, Mr. Kaminker. As mentioned, he was fully convinced that simultaneous extempore translation as Dostert wanted it was extremely difficult, if not absolutely impossible. He suggested a system including one successive translation and two subsequent simultaneous interpretations, the method used in Geneva, referred to earlier as "simultaneous successive interpretation." But at the IMT meeting, Colonel Gill, Jackson's executive, firmly replied that such a combination of simultaneous and consecutive interpretations was unnecessary: if two interpreters were translating from the booth, then the third did not need to "stand up."[44]

Once Dostert arrived in Nuremberg at the end of October, he managed to create confidence in his idea. When experienced interpreters lectured him on the impossibility of interpreting simultaneously, Dostert would reply that it would work, for the simple reason that otherwise the trial would never end.[45] The same idea was expressed by Gill during the Berlin meetings of the tribunal, when he considered the alternative to simultaneous interpreting, that is, three consecutive interpretations: "I do not expect to live that long—for the end of the trial."[46]

It soon became obvious that the decision to use simultaneous interpreting was the right choice: all other solutions promised only to hamper the proceedings. But the actual implementation of the project was going to be even more difficult than the decision to use it: the organizers needed the equipment and needed to have it installed quickly; they also had to find qualified interpreters to run the system. The U.S. Office Chief of Counsel, charged with the organization of the trial, set its staff for this job.

Supply and Installation of IBM Equipment

The next step after the decision to use simultaneous interpretation was to find the necessary equipment and install it. Ensign William Jackson, Justice Jackson's son, contacted IBM to provide the equipment. He had been at the League of Nations and probably learned there that in Geneva and at other international conferences, IBM had installed equipment (the Filene-Finlay system) that could be used for simultaneous interpreting. IBM answered him via mail on August 8, 1945. They sent information about their "International Translator System" based on the Filene-Finlay patents. Their letter includes a description of the system, drawings and a picture of the installation.

They informed him that they were ready to deliver the system immediately, together with 200 headphones and the necessary cables. They were willing to supply it at no cost provided that transportation was paid for by the government.[47]

In his memoirs, the British Chief Prosecutor, Sir David Maxwell-Fyfe, praises the generosity of IBM in supplying the equipment for free, on a loan basis.[48] According to IBM, "This was part of [their] program to bring about international understanding and promote 'World Peace Through World Trade.'"[49] For others it had nothing to do with generosity and peace:

> This was an outstanding example of a "loss leader." Thanks to the great success of the system at Nuremberg, IBM were later able to sell it to the United Nations in New York.[50]

IBM also informed Ensign Jackson he would need skilled personnel to install the system. They suggested that two engineers from Jackson's staff be trained at IBM premises two days before shipment of material. Later telegrams from Ensign Jackson show that the two engineers were sent to IBM and that they supervised the installation of the equipment at Nuremberg. IBM also sent some engineers from their staff, who worked together with U.S. Army Signal Corps technicians. All the technicians were headed by Major Vincent, the engineer in charge of the technical aspects of the interpreting system throughout the trial. He had worked for IBM before the trial and returned to this company afterwards.[51] Finally, about three weeks before the beginning of the trial, an Army aircraft with a cargo of six crates containing the interpreting equipment landed in Nuremberg, together with the IBM engineers. The installation began immediately.

The major problem in setting up the interpreting system was time. The equipment arrived at the end of October 1945, and the opening of the trial had been set for November 20. As soon as he arrived in Nuremberg, Colonel Dostert started pressing Captain Daniel U. Kiley, architect and restorer of the *Justizpalast* where the trial was going to be held, to have the equipment installed as soon as possible because he needed it for testing and training interpreters.

The main obstacle was that the *Justizpalast* had been badly damaged during the war and its restoration proceeded slowly. During the restoration works, part of the floor of the courtroom collapsed three stories into the basement, killing two workers. This prevented an early definitive installation of the simultaneous equipment, and a provisional installation was made in the attic of the courthouse, one floor above the courtroom.

Moreover, in August 1945 IBM were only able to provide for 200 headphones but the courtroom in Nuremberg needed many more. The problem was solved when Gill, of the U.S. Office Chief of Counsel, located 300 earphones for the interpreting equipment in Geneva. He organized to have them picked up on September 19, 1945 and delivered to Nuremberg around September 22.[52]

The time pressure started to become high. Only three weeks were left before the beginning of what was going to be the most important trial in history. Yet one thing was still missing, a crucial element for the trial to take place: simultaneous interpreters.

Recruitment of the Interpreting Personnel

Recruiting interpreters for Nuremberg was a two-step process. Candidates were tested for language skills in their home countries. The selected candidates were then sent to Nuremberg, where Dostert would test them for simultaneous interpreting. The criteria for selection were very strict because of the difficulty of the job. Hence, not only was it extremely hard to find people to be selected for Nuremberg; of those selected, only a few became interpreters.

Initial Recruiting at the Pentagon.   The recruitment process started in the U.S. because this was the nation organizing and financing the language services. The very first step for the recruiting of all Nuremberg personnel was laid down in an Executive Order of U.S. President Harry Truman. Dated May 2, 1945, it appointed Robert H. Jackson representative of the U.S. in the prosecution and gave him the power to hire all necessary personnel.[53]

After Dostert's idea of simultaneous interpreting was accepted, Mr. Suro, Chief Translator at the State Department, laid out a plan for the language services at the Nuremberg Trial. It was based on the UN multilanguage conference that the State Department had recently organized in San Francisco, and it contemplated an interpreting, a translating and a reporting bureau. The plan required six interpreters for each of four languages, plus an administrative officer in the interpreting division, and 12 translators plus nine stenographers for each language. In addition, before the beginning of the trial, a number of interpreters, stenographers and translators would be needed for pretrial interrogations and for translating the huge bulk of German captured documents.

Following this plan and drawing their authorization from Truman's Executive Order, the State and War departments started an all-out effort to recruit the personnel needed in Nuremberg. The War

Department was responsible for recruiting enlisted personnel. Civilian personnel were hired either through the State Department or the War Department Civilian Personnel, Overseas Division.[54] All the departments encountered difficulties in the recruiting process. First of all, military personnel were hired and sent to Nuremberg easily because they did not need visas and passports, but the Executive Order did not work well for the recruitment of civilians, because their departure to Nuremberg was conditional on the procurement of travel documents. To eliminate the delay, Jackson's staff in Europe repeatedly requested that passport requirements be waived for civilian interpreters and translators so desperately needed in Nuremberg.[55]

A contribution to a swifter recruiting process was given by Truman on September 24, 1945. He issued another Executive Order appointing Judges Biddle and Parker as Member and Alternate Member of the Nuremberg bench respectively, and also included a paragraph on the issue of recruiting:

> The Secretary of State, the Secretary of War, the Attorney General, and the Secretary of the Navy are authorized to provide appropriate assistance to the Member and the Alternate Member... and may assign or detail such personnel, including members of the armed forces, as may be requested for the purpose.[56]

Still, other problems arose. A telegram from the War Department of September 17, 1945 reports that the State Department had difficulties in finding competent translators for German, French and Russian, and urged recruitment in theater and from Great Britain.[57] Their major problem was the supply of German-speaking personnel. It was still not clear at that point whether it was possible to recruit Germans for the Nuremberg positions, especially for court reporting. A possible alternative was to employ Austrians and Swiss.[58] The Personnel List of the Translation Division shows that later on German court reporters were hired; the list names 17.

Finally, another difficulty slowed the recruiting process. The War Department was not in a position to judge the abilities of the translator and interpreter candidates. Charles Horsky, Jackson's executive in Washington, suggested that this task be handed over to the State Department, in the person of the Chief Translator, Mr. Suro. The State Department was considered more qualified for testing and hiring language personnel; because of the UN international conference they had recently organized in San Francisco, they were informed about translation procedures, personnel requirements and fees.[59] Following this suggestion, Mr. Suro was put in charge of providing the interpreters and translators for translation into German and English.[60]

These solutions accelerated the recruiting process in the U.S., but other allied nations had to provide their personnel, too. Thus, while his staff in Washington were hiring and testing personnel, Jackson informed other delegations in Europe of what they were expected to do. Already on August 31, 1945 in London, Jackson outlined Suro's plan for language services to the other delegations. France and Russia would have to provide personnel for translation, interpretation and court reporting into French and Russian respectively. The U.S. and Great Britain would share the responsibility for the English and German languages. Jackson requested each country to provide six interpreters, 12 translators and nine stenographers. The French, British and Russian delegations committed themselves to finding the necessary personnel.

However, their commitment did not seem to be enough for Jackson. A month later, he was still very much concerned about the recruitment of interpreters. He was confident that the Americans would be able to recruit personnel for translation into English and German from all other languages, but he doubted that the French and the Russians would be able to do so for their languages. The American delegation was so positive that a four-language trial would not be feasible that they already envisaged two alternatives:

    a. a waiver of the four-language requirement: each prosecuting team would present their case in their language and the only translation would be into German for the use of the defendants.

    b. a two-language trial, English and German, conducted by the British and the Americans.[61]

However, such radical alternatives were not needed. On October 2, 1945, Great Britain, France and Russia committed themselves again to provide qualified interpreting personnel,[62] while in the U.S., the initial problems had been ironed out, and considerable steps forward were being undertaken.

The Test at the Pentagon.   The first step in the selection process consisted in a language test carried out at the Pentagon. In the U.S., Mr. Suro, the Chief Translator, who was in charge of selecting the language personnel to be sent to Nuremberg, decided to appoint someone to supervise the selection and to hire the personnel. Obviously, the most experienced, best qualified person to handle the task was Léon Dostert, who had devised and promoted the simultaneous interpreting system in the first place.

In the meantime, however, Dostert had accepted a new assignment at the War Department, namely the writing of the history of Civil

Affairs. Efforts were made from Europe and from Washington to have him removed from that assignment and to secure him for the supervision of language personnel recruitment.[63] Dostert finally assumed the command of the hiring process in the U.S. on October 1, 1945.[64] He decided to administer tests for general language knowledge in Washington and to ship the selected candidates to Nuremberg.

The people who showed up at his office at the Pentagon to be tested as translators, interpreters or stenographers had learned about the Nuremberg positions in many different ways. The two Executive Orders of Truman had been circulated among the branches of the U.S. government and thus the people working in government offices and for the Army were informed of the incoming trials. Army personnel were requisitioned through the Army or the Defense Department and were sent to Nuremberg on Temporary Duty for 90 days. The civilians who reported to Dostert's office had heard about the trial and the need for language personnel through the wide newspaper publicity given to the upcoming event. Of the Nuremberg interpreters who were interviewed during the research for this book, Edith Coliver heard about the trials through the newspaper while working in Washington. She applied to the War Department and was interviewed by them.[65] Peter Uiberall was informed by his wife, who was serving in the Army and was stationed near Frankfurt in Germany. A native speaker of German, Uiberall reported to Dostert and was hired by him.[66] Alfred Steer, a scholar of German literature, heard of the trials from a military officer in a bar in Washington, D.C., who advised him to go to the Pentagon and see Dostert.[67]

Mr. Steer recalls the German test he had to take at the Pentagon.[68] He was required to translate a news clip into German. He was somewhat annoyed at this because he was fluent in German, and Dostert, who was administering the test, could not speak that language. But Dostert explained that it was the normal procedure to fend off curiosity-seekers and tourists. Maybe because of his scarce knowledge of German, Dostert realized he needed a native speaker to conduct the language test at the Pentagon. Thus, when Peter Uiberall showed up, Dostert appointed him for this task.

In order to test the candidates, Uiberall would ask them to name 10 trees, 10 automobile parts, 10 agricultural implements, etc., in two languages. He was testing not only general language knowledge: his tests were job-oriented, since interpreters were required to be knowledgeable about a variety of fields and to master the corresponding vocabulary in the languages they wanted to work in. He remembers his surprise at the number of city people who could not name agricultural implements in their native language.[69]

The candidates selected for their language skills were shipped to Nuremberg. The first batch of 10 to 15 of the 69 interpreters and translators who were to work at the trial were sent at the beginning of October 1945. They were needed to conduct the pretrial interrogations. Throughout October the recruiting process went on and more and more language personnel were transferred to Europe.

At the end of October, Dostert decided it was time to leave Washington for Europe: the IBM equipment was to arrive soon in Nuremberg, and he had to supervise its installation. The interpreters also needed to be trained. With only three weeks left before the beginning of the trial, a lot of work still needed to be done from Nuremberg. Dostert put his office in charge of continuing to select and send people to Nuremberg; together with his staff, he landed in Europe and reached Nuremberg on October 29, 1945. He reported for duty on October 31, 1945.

The Recruitment Process in Europe.   In the meantime in Europe, recruiting the interpreting personnel was still a cause of much concern. Jackson's fears that France and Russia would not be able to provide their personnel proved to be founded. On October 29, 1945, only 22 days before the opening of the trial, no French or Russian interpreter or translator had shown up in Nuremberg. As a matter of fact, Americans were the only delegation conducting pretrial interrogations. The British chose not to interrogate, but the French and the Russians simply did not have enough interpreters.[70]

The issue of language personnel was once again raised at the IMT meeting of the judges on October 29, 1945. Gill requested each delegation to hire a minimum of four court reporters, six interpreters and six translators.[71] The French delegation, for instance, had to provide six interpreters into French, two for each of the other languages to translate from. The American Judge Biddle objected that this number might be insufficient to provide all the language services needed, but he was assured that 64 people, including court reporters, would suffice. In fact Biddle was right; shortly before the start of the trial it turned out that 36 interpreters would be needed instead of 24, and that the amount of documents to be translated exceeded what 24 translators could handle. During the trial, interpreters and translators (excluding the Russian team) amounted to almost 300,[72] and the long Personnel List of the Translation Division confirms that Gill was greatly underestimating the tribunal's needs for language services.

At the October 29, 1945 IMT meeting, Gill also explained to the other delegations that the system would only work if three requirements would be met. First, the mechanical equipment had to be efficient; Gill had no fear about it, because he considered the U.S. Army Signal Corps to be completely qualified for this job. Second, the whole court had to be disciplined in speaking: people had to speak slowly and one at a time. Finally, the system would only work if every delegation recruited top-notch interpreters.[73] It was also important, he insisted, to have the interpreters ready at the beginning of November (no later than November 10). The task for the Allied nations was therefore not easy: they not only had to provide the personnel quickly, but also had to select high caliber personnel. The French, British and Russian delegations finally announced the results of their recruiting efforts. The Russian Judge Nikitchenko said that the Russian team was being recruited from England, Germany and France. The French delegation assured that the interpreters into French would arrive in Nuremberg by November 7 or 8. Finally, Judge Lawrence of the British delegation confirmed the arrival of the British interpreting team for November 7, 1945.

Once in Europe, Dostert and his staff continued to hire personnel. They knew that most of the personnel recruited so far was borrowed from other agencies, or had left their professions on leave of absence; after their time expired, they would have to leave. Later on during the trial, when many Americans had to go back to their country, this problem was solved by replacing them with French, Dutch and Swiss, that is, people recruited directly in Europe. In order to find and recruit personnel, Dostert sent Alfred Steer, who had become his deputy, all over Europe. IBM suggested contacting their office in Geneva, which would be able to assist in providing trained translating personnel. Steer also went to the League of Nations in Geneva, but he found that the interpreters there were older and accustomed to reading pre-translated texts, so that it was not certain whether they would be able to stand the strain of simultaneous interpretation. He found good candidates in smaller countries such as Belgium and Holland, where people generally speak one or more foreign languages with ease. He also discovered that the Paris Telephone Exchange was a good place to pick interpreters, because the people working there were used to translating daily conversations simultaneously over the phone.[74]

Testing and Hiring Interpreters in Nuremberg.   All the people who passed the language tests administered in Washington, D.C. or by their respective governments were sent to Nuremberg for the second part of the hiring process. Selection in the first part of the process did not imply that they could interpret simultaneously. The potential interpreters were given extensive testing in order to determine if they were actually able to listen and translate at the same time. The tests were given regardless of nationality, that is, into-German interpreters could be French or British nationals, as long as they mastered the German language.

The interpreting test consisted of a mock trial situation in which the potential interpreters were put in the booth and had to interpret simultaneously into their mother tongue or the language with which they felt most comfortable. In these mock trials, some people played the judges, some the prosecutors, etc., and they read documents or improvised speeches according to what they thought a real trial would look like. It was easy to determine which candidates could translate simultaneously and which could not stand the nervous strain. Speed was the acid test. The pace of reading was increased gradually to reach normal and then fast speech. If interpreters could not handle normal speed of discourse, they would not be suited for the job.

The mock trials for testing personnel were carried out in the attic of the Palace of Justice, where a provisional interpreting system had been installed by Dostert and Major Vincent. Eventually, when the war-damage repairs of the courthouse were completed, the interpreting system was installed in the courtroom, and the mock trials were held there.[75]

Criteria of Selection.   Simultaneous interpreting, in the form it was to take, had not existed before the Nuremberg trial. Thus, there were no established criteria according to which the candidates could be judged. Alfred Steer and Peter Uiberall, who at some point were in charge of selecting and testing interpreters, figured that the basic requirements would be similar to those for consecutive interpreting: an exceptional knowledge of the two languages and a broad cultural and educational background. In addition, candidates needed specific qualifications for simultaneous interpreting, such as composure and the ability to remain calm in stressful situations.

As far as language was concerned, interpreters were supposed to have a native-like knowledge of the foreign language(s) with which they wanted to work. The language mastery and fluency had to be accompanied by a broad vocabulary in many different subjects such as law, medicine and current affairs. It was thought that greater mastery and fluency were needed for interpreting *into* a language rather than *from* it, and therefore the Translation Division[76] was looking for people with a consistent and recent experience with the foreign language (for the interpreters translating into a foreign language).[77]

Linguistic ability by itself did not ensure interpreting proficiency. High levels of culture and education were required. The interpreters' background had to be broad enough to include "a wide range
of vocabulary and an ability to assimilate a variety of subjects."[78] The
best results were achieved when the interpreters had spent several years
in the countries of both languages: for instance, if they had received
their education in the native country and had professional experience in
a foreign country.[79] Other criteria that indicated good candidates for
interpreting were a professional background in law and public speaking
experience.[80]

Finally, the Translation Division was looking for skills that were
required specifically for simultaneous interpreting. Given the stressful
conditions of the job, interpreters had to have self-composure under pressure and the ability to concentrate in difficult situations. The job required
the mental agility to hear and speak at the same time, and to adapt instantaneously to the stimulus of the source language. This means that interpreters had to be able to quickly find an alternative if the best translation
did not come to mind, as they were not supposed to stutter or stop. They
had to be able to make decisions quickly and accurately. The job also
required great mental and physical efforts because of the need to interpret
both speedily and accurately, and to adapt to the speed of the speaker.
Finally, interpreters were required to have a good voice and clear enunci-
ation, so that it would be easy to listen to them for hours at a time. It is
reported that the division removed "several interpreters whose speech
habits made listening to them most uncomfortable in the long run."[81]

Results of Selection.   The division started selecting people who
met these criteria, and found out that the best interpreters were usually
between 35 and 45. Younger people lacked the vocabulary and older
ones could not stand the strain of the job. Moreover, men usually had
better voices than women but, according to Steer, "when women are
good they are very good indeed."[82] Also, bilingual people were preferred to people speaking many languages, because it turned out that
the mastery of the language decreases proportionally to the number of
languages known.[83] They also found out that true bilingualism is rare,
as there are always slight differences between the languages one
speaks.[84] Steer did not believe in real bilingualism: "Occasionally
someone would show up who claimed two mother tongues. We settled
this by having him identify all the kitchen utensils, which only a child
watching his mother would learn."[85]

It was also found out that, although many interpreters preferred
to translate into their mother tongue, "the best work was done when the

interpreter listened to his native tongue and translated into the second language... The interpreter first had to understand perfectly what was being said and then could usually find suitable words in the second language to express the thought."[86] As Mr. Uiberall recalls:

> We preferred people like Wolfe Frank [German-into-English interpreter], who had native tongue German but who had lived long enough in an English-speaking country and had enough experience with the English language, in different fields of profession and endeavors.[87]

Not everyone agreed, though. According to Alfred Steer, translating from one's mother tongue provides a better translation in terms of understanding and meaning, but it lacks in terms of delivery, since the pronunciation often sounds foreign to the listeners. Translating *into* one's mother tongue "eliminates the problem of accents which the microphone seems to exaggerate,"[88] while the non-native ability to speak the language reduces the possibilities of a refined and elegant delivery. People "possess superior vocabulary and superior fluency in their mother tongue."[89] Despite this, it turned out that the best interpreters were those who translated from their mother tongue into a language they knew extremely well, like Wolfe Frank.

Finally, the division discovered that many linguists with excellent academic backgrounds could not do the job because, even though they could translate Schopenhauer, they could not cope with subjects like toilet arrangements in concentration camps. For this reason the best academic linguists and translators were sometimes refused for the job.

Basically, the division discovered that few, very few people could do simultaneous interpreting. Alfred Steer, who in a year tested more than 400 people, calculated that only five percent of the people tested, including experienced consecutive interpreters, could do simultaneous interpreting. More than 200 people were tested before the trial to obtain the first 36 simultaneous interpreters. In all, more than 500 sat for the interpreting test during the trial. Soon after the testing started it was realized what a difficult task was required of a simultaneous interpreter:

> The vital thing everyone agrees upon is that simultaneous translation requires translators of a degree and skill far beyond that of the average translator or interpreter.[90]

The low percentage of interpreters selected was certainly due to the difficulty of the job, but also to the fact that none of the people taking the test had ever been trained for simultaneous interpreting. Thus the percentage of people who could translate simultaneously was extremely low, differently from today, because they were improvising. Because of this reason and because of a desperate need for interpreting personnel throughout the trial, some of the standards were later relaxed, and some interpreters were criticized and replaced for their poor performance.[91]

From the onset, Dostert decided to test the linguists that the division had already hired as translators or Interrogation Division interpreters (who worked consecutively sentence by sentence). It was thought that they might be able to perform well, since they had been working with the terminology of the trial and had had time to become familiar with it. These people were constantly invited to try out a mock trial situation, in order to see if they could perform well over the microphone. A lot of them did not even try, many were not able to do simultaneous interpreting, but in the end, the core of the first simultaneous interpreters was drawn from the pretrial interrogation interpreters and document translators.

Training. The interpreters selected to work in the courtroom were given training sessions in the form of mock trials. They practiced with the provisional installation of the simultaneous interpreting equipment set in the attic. Here they would read documents to each other and improvise prosecutors' and judges' speeches while some of them would be interpreting. The speed of speech was increased gradually and the voice, facility of speech and performance of the interpreter were checked and corrected. The training program usually lasted two weeks to one or two months, but exceptionally some people were put in the courtroom with only a few days training (especially later during the trial, when the time pressure became higher). Elisabeth Heyward, for example, remembers receiving no training at all.[92] During these mock trials interpreters were also instructed on how to improve their linguistic performance. Their deliveries were recorded and checked in order to correct mistakes in pronunciation (for interpreters working into a foreign language). The training program continued throughout the trial as more and more interpreter candidates were selected.

As mentioned, many of the people who took the interpreting test were not able to do simultaneous interpreting. This revealed the inefficiency of the double selection system. In Nuremberg, Dostert and Steer faced the mounting problem that the new batches of people sent by the Pentagon were mostly ill-prepared. They had been selected because they could speak two languages or had a language degree, but once in Nuremberg they could not do simultaneous interpreting. Some of them were employed for written translation. If they showed some ability, such as administration, editing, etc., they were hired in that capacity. Of the people who did not test out as interpreters, for example, Alfred Steer became Dostert's assistant, Marguerite Wolf was employed as

Head of the Transcript Reviewing Branch and Major Lawrence Egbert was given the task of compiling a glossary of legal terms in different languages.[93]

The great majority, however, had no other skill and was of no use in Nuremberg, and the division had to find a diplomatic way to get rid of these people. "The rejects were consigned to an area called 'Siberia,' performing menial tasks until they could be shipped back" to their country of origin.[94]

Dress Rehearsals.   Although the equipment had been installed and interpreters were being selected and trained, before the beginning of the trial there was still much concern and uneasiness about simultaneous interpreting. Members of the court were still skeptical about the system and doubted that it would work at all. Thus the Allied delegations agreed to organize at least one dress rehearsal, to make sure that the system was working properly and that the interpreters were actually able to translate simultaneously.[95] Judge Biddle proposed to hold at least two full-scale rehearsals, with judges, prosecutors, defense, interpreters and reporters in the last week before the trial.

Conversely, the interpreting staff was worried that the members of the court would prevent the system from working because *they* did not know how to use it. Thus they welcomed the idea of a dress rehearsal, in which they could show the court the functioning of the system. Jackson fully agreed that the court needed training too, and he repeatedly stressed the need for everyone to practice with the system and to become familiar with it.[96]

The first dress rehearsal took place on November 5, 1945, but not in the actual courtroom, which was still being repaired. Jackson made accurate checks of the interpreting system and a few problems were ironed out. Only nine interpreters were present at this mock trial, because the Russians did not show up.[97] This was the first of a series of rehearsals in which the system and the personnel were completely tested out. At one of these rehearsals, Dostert and his staff staged a mock trial where they played the different roles, showing the real "actors" how to use the microphone, how fast to speak, etc. Mr. Steer, Dostert's deputy, remembers playing the presiding judge at this mock trial.[98]

The Translation Division

The interpreters and translators of the Western nations were pooled into the Translation Division of the U.S. Office, Chief of Counsel for War Crimes (OCCWC), which was divided into Court Interpreting Branch,

Translating Branch, Court Reporting Branch and Transcript Reviewing Branch. Other branches were Recording and Printing. The Translation Division was headed by Léon Dostert and taken over by his Executive Officer, Alfred Steer, after Dostert left for the United Nations in April 1946. Dostert's Executive Officers were, besides Steer, Joachim von Zastrow and Peter Uiberall. Dostert was also Chief Interpreter. The people in charge of the other delegations' interpreting teams were: André Kaminker for the French team, Mr. Sinclair for the British team and General Rudenko (the Russian Prosecutor) for the Russian team.[99] From the beginning it had been decided that the Translation Division would have a U.S. director and three deputy directors from the other countries.[100] The Translating Branch was headed by William H. Mercer, "a distinguished, multi-lingual British Foreign Service officer."[101] Joachim von Zastrow, who occasionally worked as monitor, was the Head of the Court Reporting Branch and of the Interpreting Branch for a while, and Marguerite Wolf, British, headed the Transcript Reviewing Branch.

The Translation Division was organized as follows:

I. Court Interpreting Branch
  A. Simultaneous court interpreters. Three teams of 12 people.
  B. Auxiliary consecutive interpreters. About 12 people. Used for languages different than the languages of the tribunal, such as Polish, and Yiddish. Two bench interpreters sitting behind the judges and translating their consultations.

II. Translating Branch

  Eight sections of 20 to 25 people. Each section was assigned a specific one-way direction of translation, for example, Russian into French. Since it was hard to find people who could write elegant and literate prose, 15 or 18 translators would do the job roughly, and about eight would edit the translations, review and polish the language. These people were called "editors" or "reviewers." Every translation section had a typing pool consisting of five to 10 typists who copied handwritten translations into typescripts.

III. Court Reporting Branch

  About 12 people for each language. They worked a half-hour shift recording original speeches in their language and the translations into their language.

IV. Transcript Reviewing Branch

  The reviewing section consisted of about 100 people of all languages, who were hired subsequently when the idea of printing the proceedings was adopted. These people reviewed the short-hand transcripts of the translations against the verbatim record-ing of the original speech.

Pretrial arrangements ended shortly before the beginning of the trial. The equipment had been installed, the 36 necessary interpreters had been selected and trained. The court members had been instructed on how to use the system. The Translation Division was ready for the first day of the trial. It was vital for the trial that the interpreting system work well: if the system broke down, the trial would be a farce, a meaningless gathering of people who could not understand each other. Considering the effort everyone had put into installing, recruiting, training and practicing, the division was quite sure that interpreting would not fail. But last-minute hitches were always possible.

On November 19, 1945 mock trials and training sessions stopped. The following day, interpreting would begin for real.

Notes

1. For a discussion of the spelling of the word "Nuremberg," see Glossary and Defi-nitions.
2. See Appendix for a list of the defendants.
3. See Appendix for more details on defendants' counts, verdicts and sentences.
4. For a description of these techniques, see Glossary and Definitions.
5. Jean Herbert, "How Conference Interpreting Grew." *Language Interpretation and Communication.* Ed. by D. Gerver and Wallace H. Sinaiko (New York: Plenum, 1978): 5. Created in 1874, the World Postal Union (WPU) holds congresses every five years. Important congresses that resulted in conventions before the First World War were held in 1885, 1891, 1987, 1906 and 1920. Membership is open to every state in the world.
6. These commissions were set up after the Armistice had been signed to discuss all sorts of subjects between the representatives of the German Army and those of the Allied and Associated Forces, as they were called. (Jean Herbert, "How Confer-ence Interpreting Grew." *Language Interpretation and Communication.* Ed. by D. Gerver and Wallace H. Sinaiko [New York: Plenum, 1978]: 6.)
7. Jean Herbert, "How Conference Interpreting Grew." *Language Interpretation and Communication.* Ed. by D. Gerver and Wallace H. Sinaiko (New York: Plenum, 1978): 5.
8. Université de Genève, "Conference Interpretation at the École de Traduction et d'Interprétation" (leaflet) and "École d'Interprètes." *L'Interprète* 4 (1952): 10.
9. "Information Concerning Interpreters" (ts. Spring 1946).
10. AIIC, *The Interpreters: A Historical Perspective*, videocassette.
11. Dana Schmidt, "Pick Your Language." *The New York Times Magazine* 6 (Aug. 25, 1946): 24.

12. Marie-France Skuncke, "Tout a commencé à Nuremberg." *Parallèles* 11 (1989): 7.

13. Marianne Lederer, *La traduction simultanée: expérience et théorie* (Paris: Lettres Modernes, 1981): 16.

14. André Kaminker, "Conférence prononcée à l'Université de Genève." *L'Interprète* 10, 3 and 4 (1955): 11-12. "Simultaneous interpretation is not new. It has been used for a long time. In 1926 or 1927 a man called Filene... invented simultaneous interpretation together with an engineer called Finlay. Filene was the one who thought that it could be possible to listen and translate at the same time. They contacted Mr. Watson, the president of IBM. The three men obtained a patent for the invention. I still wonder how they managed to get a patent because in fact they did not invent anything. The fact of putting together a microphone and three or four channels connected to each other can hardly be considered an invention." My translation.

15. International Business Machine Corporation, "That All Men May Understand" (ts. n.d.).

16. Gilbert Bourgain, "A Genève, retour de Nuremberg." *AIIC Bulletin* 19.4 (1991): 18. Qtd. in Ruth Morris, "Technology and the Worlds of Interpreting." In *Future and Communication: The Role of Scientific and Technical Communication and Translation in Technology Development and Transfer*. International Scholars Publications. Ed. by Y. Gitay and D. Porush (San Francisco: Rousenhouse, 1997): 177-184.

17. Hilary Gaskin, ed., *Eyewitnesses at Nuremberg* (London: Arms, 1990): 43.

18. "Telephonic Interpretation—The System of the Future?" *L'Interprète* 1.5 (August/ September 1946): 2-4.

19. Henri van Hoof, *Théorie et pratique de l'interprétation: avec application particulière à l'anglais et au français* (Munich: Max Hueber Verlag, 1962): 19.

20. Participant to the AIIC conference (AIIC, *Nurnberg*, Geneva 1992, videocassette). Ivan Petrovic Pavlov, 1849-1936, Russian physiologist, won the Nobel Prize for Physiology in 1904.

21. Gelij V. Chernov, "Conference Interpretation in the U.S.S.R.: History, Theory, New Frontiers." *Meta* 37.1 (1992): 149. Qtd. in Ruth Morris, "Technology and the Worlds of Interpreting." In *Future and Communication: The Role of Scientific and Technical Communication and Translation in Technology Development and Transfer*. International Scholars Publications. Ed. by Y. Gitay and D. Porush (San Francisco: Rousenhouse, 1997): 177-184. One source indicates the use of five languages while others only report French, English, German and Russian.

22. Participant to the AIIC conference (AIIC, *Nurnberg*, Geneva 1992, videocassette). For additional details about the use of simultaneous interpreting equipment in different countries before 1945, see Ruth Morris, "Technology and the Worlds of Interpreting." In *Future and Communication: The Role of Scientific and Technical Communication and Translation in Technology Development and Transfer*. International Scholars Publications. Ed. by Y. Gitay and D. Porush (San Francisco: Rousenhouse, 1997): 177-184.

23. Léon Dostert, "The Instantaneous Multi-Lingual Interpreting System in the International Military Tribunal" (ts. n.d.): 1.

24. Léon Dostert, "The Instantaneous Multi-Lingual Interpreting System in the International Military Tribunal" (ts. n.d.): 2.

25. Ann and John Tusa, *The Nuremberg Trial* (London: Macmillan, 1983); Francis Biddle, *In Brief Authority* (Garden City: Doubleday, 1962); "Great Nuremberg

Trial Opens." *The New York Times* (Nov. 21, 1945); David and Margareta Bowen, "The Nuremberg Trials: Communication through Translation." *Meta* 30, 1 (1985): 74-77.

26. Ann and John Tusa, *The Nuremberg Trial* (London: Macmillan, 1983): 218. Emphasis added.

27. "Charter of the International Military Tribunal...

    IV. FAIR TRIAL FOR DEFENDANTS...
    Article 16. In order to ensure fair trial for the Defendants, the following procedure shall be followed:...
    (c) A preliminary examination of a Defendant and his trial shall be conducted in, or translated into, a language which the defendant understands...

    V. POWERS OF THE TRIBUNAL AND CONDUCT OF THE TRIAL...
    Article 25. All official documents shall be produced, and all court proceedings conducted, in English, French, and Russian, and in the language of the Defendant. So much of the record and of the proceedings may also be translated into the language of any country in which the Tribunal is sitting, as the Tribunal considers desirable in the interests of justice and public opinion." (Jay W. Baird, ed., *From Nuremberg to My Lay* [Lexington: Heath, 1972]: 15, 17.)

28. "Charter of the International Military Tribunal...

    I. CONSTITUTION OF THE TRIBUNAL
    Article 1. ... there shall be established an International Military Tribunal... for the just and prompt trial and punishment of the major war criminals of the European Axis." (Jay W. Baird, ed., *From Nuremberg to My Lay* [Lexington: Heath, 1972]: 11.)

29. David and Margareta Bowen, "The Nuremberg Trials: Communication through Translation." *Meta* 30, 1 (1985): 75.

30. International Military Tribunal, Seventeenth Organizational Meeting (ts. Oct. 29, 1945): 3, 4, 6, 7.

31. William Jackson to the Secretary of State Byrnes, State Department Central Decimal Files 1945-1949. File No. 740.00116 EW Prosecution/10-145. Belsen is a city in Lower Saxony, famous for its prison camps during the Nazi time and the Second World War.

32. International Military Tribunal, Seventeenth Organizational Meeting (ts. Oct. 29, 1945): 16.

33. E. Peter Uiberall, letter to the author (Feb. 11, 1995).

34. See his biography in chapter 5 "Profiles of Interpreters."

35. E. Peter Uiberall, letter to the author (Feb. 11, 1995).

36. William Jackson to the Secretary of State Byrnes, "Memorandum for Secretary Byrnes" (Oct. 1, 1945) State Department Central Decimal Files 1945-1949. File No. 740.00116 EW Prosecution/10-145.

37. Charles A. Horsky, letter to the author (April 27, 1995).

38. Chief Prosecutors, Note of Meeting (ts. Aug. 31, 1945): 1.

39. Joseph E. Persico, *Nuremberg: Infamy on Trial* (New York: Viking-Penguin, 1994): 53-54.

40. Charles A. Horsky, "Memorandum for Mr. Justice Jackson" (ts. Sept. 5, 1945).

41. Chief Prosecutors, Note of Meeting (ts. Aug. 31, 1945): 1.

42. International Military Tribunal, Seventeenth Organizational Meeting (ts. Oct. 29, 1945): 16.

43. André Kaminker, "Conférence prononcée à l'Université de Genève." *L'Interprète* 10, 3 and 4 (1955): 10. "Simultaneous interpretation was introduced at Nuremberg even though, allow me to say, the trial seemed to be the least suitable place for simultaneous interpretation. The defendants' lives were at stake, and it was impossible for them to listen to the interpretation and check its accuracy while testifying. Which is, of course, one of the major shortcomings of simultaneous interpretation." My translation.

44. International Military Tribunal, Seventeenth Organizational Meeting (ts. Oct. 29, 1945): 12. It is obvious from Gill's remark that he did not understand the difference between the two methods. It is not just that "two [interpreters] sit down and one stands up," as he said, but that with the combined method all the interpretations are consecutive, not simultaneous, to the original speech. The difference in delivery and accuracy can be remarkable.

45. Marie-France Skuncke, Conference (AIIC, *Nurnberg*, Geneva 1992, videocassette).

46. International Military Tribunal, Seventeenth Organizational Meeting (ts. Oct. 29, 1945): 11.

47. Anderson to William E. Jackson, letter (ts. Aug. 8, 1945).

48. David Maxwell-Fyfe Kilmuir, *Political Adventure: The Memoirs of the Earl of Kilmuir* (London: Weidenfeld, 1964): 97.

49. A.C. Holt, "International Understanding: A Tribute to Mr. Thomas J. Watson" (ts. n.d.): 2.

50. Ann and John Tusa, *The Nuremberg Trial* (London: Macmillan, 1983): 110.

51. E. Peter Uiberall, letter to the author (Feb. 11, 1995).

52. Gill for Jackson, telegram 1128 (ts. Sept. 22, 1945).

53. Harry S. Truman, Executive Order 9547, *Code of Federal Regulations* 3, 2, 1943-1948 (Washington, D.C.: Government Printing Office, 1951).

54. "Record of Telephone Conference" (ts. Oct. 1, 1945): 1.

55. William Jackson to the Secretary of State Byrnes, "Memorandum for Secretary Byrnes" (Oct. 1, 1945) State Department Central Decimal Files 1945-1949. File No. 740.00116 EW Prosecution/10-145.

56. Harry S Truman, Executive Order 9626, *Code of Federal Regulations* 3, 2, 1943-1948 (Washington, D.C.: Government Printing Office, 1951).

57. War Department to Office of Chief of Counsel, Nurnberg, Telegram 1322147 (ts. Sept. 17, 1945).

58. Charles A. Horsky, "Memorandum for Mr. Justice Jackson" (ts. Sept. 5, 1945): 3.

59. Charles A. Horsky, "Memorandum for Mr. Justice Jackson" (ts. Sept. 5, 1945): 4.

60. William Jackson to the Secretary of State Byrnes, "Memorandum for Secretary Byrnes" (Oct. 1, 1945) State Department Central Decimal Files 1945-1949. File No. 740.00116 EW Prosecution/10-145.

61. William Jackson to the Secretary of State Byrnes, "Memorandum for Secretary Byrnes" (Oct. 1, 1945) State Department Central Decimal Files 1945-1949. File No. 740.00116 EW Prosecution/10-145.

62. "Record of Telephone Conference" (ts. Oct. 2, 1945).

63. Robert J. Gill to John W. Griggs, U.S. Office Chief of Counsel, Washington, D.C., "Re: Personnel for Interpreting and Translation Division." Letter (ts. Sept. 26, 1945).

64. "Record of Telephone Conference" (ts. Oct. 1, 1945): 2.

65. Edith Coliver, letter to the author (Aug. 2, 1995).

66. Hilary Gaskin, ed., *Eyewitnesses at Nuremberg* (London: Arms, 1990): 12.

67. Hilary Gaskin, ed., *Eyewitnesses at Nuremberg* (London: Arms, 1990): 1.

68. Alfred G. Steer, "Interesting Times: Memoir of Service in U.S. Navy, 1941-1947" (ts. 1992): 229.

69. Joseph E. Persico, *Nuremberg: Infamy on Trial* (New York: Viking-Penguin, 1994): 112.

70. Ann and John Tusa, *The Nuremberg Trial* (London: Macmillan, 1983): 130.

71. International Military Tribunal, Seventeenth Organizational Meeting (ts. Oct. 29, 1945): 10.

72. Dana A. Schmidt, "Pick Your Language." *The New York Times Magazine* 6 (Aug. 25, 1946).

73. International Military Tribunal, Seventeenth Organizational Meeting (ts. Oct. 29, 1945): 16.

74. The recruiting process went on throughout the trial, because of the huge personnel turnover, which was calculated to be 104 percent during the first year of the trial. Alfred G. Steer, "Interesting Times: Memoir of Service in U.S. Navy, 1941-1947" (ts. 1992): 229.

75. Images of a mock trial in the courtroom can be seen in a newsreel of 1945 (AIIC, *Nurnberg*, Geneva 1992, videocassette).

76. Dostert's staff were testing and hiring personnel not only from and for the U.S., they were also selecting personnel of other delegations for translation into French, Russian and German. In order to better coordinate the efforts for the recruitment of the first 36 interpreters, the three Western delegations of France, Great Britain and the U.S. decided to pool their personnel into a single Translation Division run by one office only. This arrangement was meant to give better results in terms of efficiency. The Soviet personnel, translators, court reporters and interpreters all responded for their job only to Russian authorities.

77. Siegfried Ramler, "Origins and Challenges of Simultaneous Interpretation: The Nuremberg Trial Experience." *Languages at Crossroads.* American Translators Association. Ed. by Deanna Lindberg Hammond (Medford: Learned Information, 1988): 438.

78. Siegfried Ramler, "Origins and Challenges of Simultaneous Interpretation: The Nuremberg Trial Experience." *Languages at Crossroads.* American Translators Association. Ed. by Deanna Lindberg Hammond (Medford: Learned Information, 1988): 438.

79. Siegfried Ramler, "Origins and Challenges of Simultaneous Interpretation: The Nuremberg Trial Experience." *Languages at Crossroads.* American Translators Association. Ed. by Deanna Lindberg Hammond (Medford: Learned Information, 1988): 438.

80. Alfred G. Steer, "Simultaneous Multi-Lingual Interpreting System" (ts. n.d.): 3, and Steer qtd. in Dana A. Schmidt, "Pick Your Language." *The New York Times Magazine* 6 (Aug. 25, 1946).

81. Alfred G. Steer, "Simultaneous Multi-Lingual Interpreting System" (ts. n.d.): 4.

82. Dana A. Schmidt, "Pick Your Language." *The New York Times Magazine* 6 (Aug. 25, 1946).

83. Léon Dostert, "The Instantaneous Multi-Lingual Interpreting System in the International Military Tribunal" (ts. n.d.): 3.

84. Siegfried Ramler, "Origins and Challenges of Simultaneous Interpretation: The Nuremberg Trial Experience." *Languages at Crossroads.* American Translators Association. Ed. by Deanna Lindberg Hammond (Medford: Learned Information, 1988): 438.

85. Alfred G. Steer, letter to the author (April 22, 1995).

86. Joseph E. Persico, *Nuremberg: Infamy on Trial* (New York: Viking-Penguin, 1994): 112.

87. Hilary Gaskin, ed., *Eyewitnesses at Nuremberg* (London: Arms, 1990): 44-45.

88. Alfred G. Steer, "Simultaneous Multi-Lingual Interpreting System" (ts. n.d.): 6.

89. Alfred G. Steer, "Simultaneous Multi-Lingual Interpreting System" (ts. n.d.): 6. There is discrepancy about this issue. According to Steer, everyone translated into their mother tongue, with a few exceptions, namely, the Russian émigrés from Paris (Alfred G. Steer, letter to the author, April 22, 1995). Mr. Uiberall, on the other hand, recalls that "at least one-half of the interpreters were translating *from* their native language," including Ramler, Dostert, Frank and himself (E. Peter Uiberall, letter to the author, Feb. 25, 1995).

90. International Military Tribunal, Seventeenth Organizational Meeting (ts. Oct. 29, 1945): 16.

91. See "Comments on Interpretation" in chapter 3.

92. Elisabeth Heyward, letter to the author (May 1, 1995).

93. Lawrence D. Egbert, Haakon M. Chevalier, and C.D. MacIntosh, "Glossary of Legal Terms French-English" (ts. n.d.).

94. Joseph E. Persico, *Nuremberg: Infamy on Trial* (New York: Viking-Penguin, 1994): 263.

95. International Military Tribunal, Seventeenth Organizational Meeting (ts. Oct. 29, 1945): 17.

96. International Military Tribunal, Seventeenth Organizational Meeting (ts. Oct. 29, 1945): 17.

97. Dana A. Schmidt, "Pick Your Language." *The New York Times Magazine* 6 (Aug. 25, 1946).

98. Alfred G. Steer, "Interesting Times: Memoir of Service in U.S. Navy, 1941-1947" (ts. 1992): 237.

99. "Interpreters" (ms. n.d.).

100. "Record of Telephone Conference" (ts. Oct. 2, 1945).

101. E. Peter Uiberall, "Court Interpreting at the Nuremberg Trial" (ts. April 11, 1995): 2.

CHAPTER TWO

DESCRIPTION OF
THE INTERPRETING SYSTEM

Finally, the day came. On November 20, 1945, the soft, calm voice of
Judge Lawrence opened the most important trial of the century. The
eyes of the world were pointed on the crowded Nuremberg courtroom, and for the first time in history they marveled at something
unknown: simultaneous interpretation. It was "what outsiders noticed
and marveled at,"[1] and "ce qui a le plus frappé les imaginations."[2]
The bizarre view of a courtroom full of people with earphones com-
peted for media and public interest with the presence of Hermann
Göring and Rudolf Hess. "One reporter thought it looked like a telephone exchange."[3]

Yet what people did not and could not know was that, beyond
the novelty of the shiny earphones, there was the anxiety of those who
had worked on the simultaneous interpreting system. They were anx-
ious to see whether their efforts would be rewarded. As the Presiding
Judge Lawrence began to speak, his words came through the cable
translated into French, German and Russian: the simultaneous interpreting system worked.

Of all the branches of the Translation Division, namely, Court
Interpreting, Translating, Reporting and Transcript Reviewing, the one
that received most attention from the media was the Interpreting Branch.
Its profound impact on both journalists of the time and, later, historians is
shown by the following quotation, in which the author sums up the four
crucial, defining elements of the trial:

> Am 14. [sic] November 1945 begann in Nürnberg vor einem interna-
> tionalen Militärtribunal der Prozeß gegen die deutschen Hauptkriegs-
> verbrecher.

Figure I—The International Military Tribunal in Nuremberg, Germany, 1945-1946. From left to right: the defendants and defense counsel. In the left corner in the back, interpreters' booths, the monitor and the Marshal of the Court. In the center, the speakers' rostrum, facing the witness box. On the right, the stenographers, the officers of the court and the Judges' Bench. On the bottom of the picture, the four tables of the Prosecution teams plus a table for court personnel. The picture is taken from the elevated gallery for the public.

Source: National Archives, College Park, MD.

Die Zahl der Angeklagten: 21, der Richter: 8, der Ankläger: 50, der Zeugen: 111, der Verteidiger: 23.

Es wurde simultan in vier Sprachen verhandelt.

Der Prozeß dauerte ein Jahr.[4]

In 1945 "it was a wonder."[5] Today, simultaneous interpreting is a daily occurrence at international meetings and conferences. Nonetheless, the Nuremberg simultaneous interpreting system, though not as sensational today as it was in 1945, is still fascinating. The system featured three teams of 12 interpreters working at four language desks. It consisted of a complex electrical transmission requiring technical assistance and was supervised by a monitor. It was a flexible system that allowed for needs such as Bench interpreting, closed session interpreting and interpretation of documents.

The Functioning of the Interpreting System

This description of the Nuremberg interpreting system is based mainly on Léon Dostert's text, "The Instantaneous Multi-Lingual Interpreting System in the International Military Tribunal." As mentioned earlier, the equipment adopted at Nuremberg was the Filene-Finlay system. The working languages were Russian, English, German and French. Everybody in the room wore earphones and every word was spoken into microphones. Every listener, judge, lawyer and press correspondent could choose the interpreted version of their choice or the original speech, called "verbatim."[6] The channel choice was possible by means of a selector switch installed at every seat and connected to the earphones. There were five channels on the dial: channel one for the verbatim speech, channel two for English, channel three carried Russian, channel four French and channel five German.

When a French prosecutor was examining a German witness, for example, the prosecutor asked a question in French. The witness heard the German translation through the earphones and answered in German into the microphone. The prosecutor heard the answer translated into French, and replied in French, and so on. At the same time an English-speaking listener heard the English version of both questions and answers. Usually, there was a pause of only a few seconds between the original and the translated versions, a pause (*décalage*) that was necessary for the interpreter to understand what he or she heard and to start translating.

The interpreters received the original speech through their earphones and translated into microphones into the language to which they were assigned. They had to speak softly in order to avoid interference with the speaker or with other interpreters, because they were sitting behind glass partitions that were open at the top. They were the only ones whose earphones were always set for the verbatim mode. Every other listener, on the other hand, selected the language of their choice.

There were 12 interpreters in the room at any time. They were divided into four desks, according to the language into which they translated. The Russian desk, for example, was made up of the German-into-Russian, the French-into-Russian and the English-into-Russian interpreters. At the French desk sat the English-French, the Russian-French and the German-French interpreters, and so on. Each desk had a microphone with an on-off switch and three headphones, and was separated from other desks by a glass panel. Obviously, only one interpreter spoke at any one time at each desk, and only three interpreters translated at any given moment in the whole courtroom.

When German was spoken, for example, the German desk was silent. Their microphone was switched off, so that the verbatim speech was carried on channel one (verbatim) and channel five (the German channel). At the other desks, only the German "experts" spoke, that is, the German-English interpreter at the English desk, the German-French interpreter at the French desk, and the German-Russian interpreter at the Russian desk. It was very important that the interpreters manipulate the on-off switch of their microphones properly. They had to know which language the speaker was going to use, so that the interpreter required at each desk would be ready on time, and the corresponding desk would be silent, that is, would switch off their microphone. If interpreters forgot to switch on their microphone, as sometimes happened, the verbatim would be carried through that channel instead of their translated version.[7] On the other hand, if the desk was supposed to be silent but the microphone was still on, nothing would be carried through that channel, with consequent loss of information for the courtroom.[8] The proper use of the switch was particularly complex during examination and cross-examination, where the lawyers and the witnesses or defendants spoke different languages, and other lawyers of the defense or prosecution intervened to make comments.

Here is an example of this complex mechanism. When a Russian prosecutor cross-examined a German witness, he asked a question in Russian. The Russian desk was silent, their microphone off. People in the room listening to the Russian channel heard the original question. On every other channel but the verbatim (channel one), listeners heard the translated version of the question, in English, French and German

Figure II—Defendants, counsel and interpreters. The Interpreters, front row: Russian and English desks; back row: German and French desks.

Source: National Archives, College Park, MD.

Figure III—Defendants, defense counsel and interpreters. Defendants, defense counsel and interpreters rise as the eight members of the Tribunal enter the courtroom. Monitors, front: Léon Dostert, back: E. Peter Uiberall and Joachim von Zastrow.

Source: National Archives, College Park, MD.

accordingly. When the witness started to answer in German, the interpreter for Russian into German quickly turned off his or her microphone, so that the original answer could be heard through channel five (the German channel). The interpreter for German into Russian turned on his or her microphone and translated the German answer into Russian. During this time, at the French and English desks, the microphones were always on, but they changed hands. At the English desk, when the witness was speaking, the German-English interpreter was translating. The latter gave the microphone to the Russian-English interpreter as soon as the prosecutor started to speak.[9] The same happened at the French desk.

Obviously, things became more complicated when a French prosecutor suddenly intervened to ask a question. Every interpreter at every time had to be ready to start translating. Because microphones had to be switched on and off every time, a pause between questions and answers was necessary, so that the interpreters translating had the time to finish the sentence before switching off the microphone. When everything worked properly, Russian-speaking people were able to follow the entire proceeding leaving their earphones set on channel three: when Russian was spoken, they heard the original speech, otherwise, they heard the translation into Russian.

As one can see in Figures II and III, interpreters were assigned specific places according to the language they interpreted into, because this allowed them to work in teams, or "language desks," and to pass the microphone to one another when necessary, and also because their microphone was connected to a specific language channel. An interpreter translating into French, therefore, could not be sitting at the Russian desk, because channel three departing from that desk was supposed to carry only Russian. Interpreters were sitting as follows (seen from the visitors' gallery),

R-G E-G F-G	R-F E-F G-F	
German Desk	French Desk	
G-R F-R E-R	R-E F-E G-E	Monitor
Russian Desk	English Desk[10]	

"The German and French desks, in the back, were elevated so that the interpreters had a clear view of the court room."[11]

As one can see from the plan of the courtroom (Fig. IV), the interpreters sat in the left rear corner of the courtroom, as seen from the visitors' gallery, between the defendants' dock and the marshal of the court. This position gave them a full view of most of the courtroom. It was, and still is, of enormous importance for an interpreter to see the

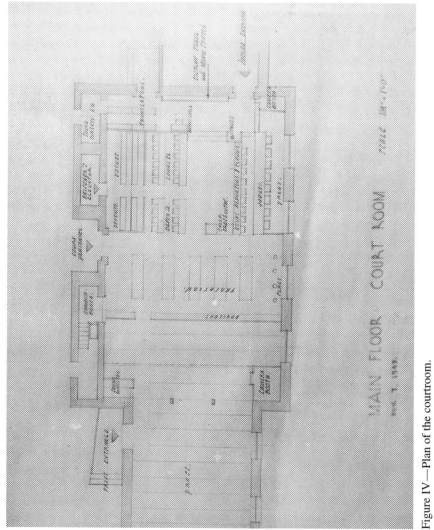

Source: National Archives, College Park, MD.

Figure IV—Plan of the courtroom.

speaker, his or her gestures, lip movements and facial expressions. This helps interpreters to fill in should they not understand one or two words, or when irony, sarcasm or similar rhetorical means are being used. This is why the partitions were made of glass, which earned the interpreters' booths the nickname "the aquarium."[12] From their position interpreters could see (right to left):

- the defendants, in profile, sitting directly in front of them. The two defendants sitting in the last seats in the front and back rows, Hans Fritzsche and Hjalmar Schacht, were close to the interpreters and observed their work with interest. Fritzsche, for example, was impressed by the performance of the interpreters and left positive comments on their work in his memoirs.[13]

- the defense counsel seen only from the back. This, however, was not a problem for interpreters because counsel were required to speak from a rostrum that was in full view. (Labeled "Chief Prosecutor" on the plan, Fig. IV, the rostrum served for both defense and prosecution.)

- court reporters and the judges, on the left, their faces in full view; the witness box, at the far left. The position of the witness stand was a problem for interpreters, who had to turn completely to their left to see the person speaking. This was easily done by the interpreters closer to the marshal but it was harder for interpreters sitting closer to the wall.

The glass panels of the interpreters' booths were open at the top. For some, this was an inconvenience because of the amount of noise they received from other interpreters and from the room. The noise coming from the courtroom was unavoidable, but interpreters at least tried to speak softly into their microphones so that they would not disturb the other desks. For Frederick Treidell, interpreter at Nuremberg, there was no extreme interference among booths. But the price to pay for it was that "on devait manger le micro pour ne pas gêner les autres... On parlait... pratiquement avec le micro dans la bouche."[14] However, the open glass partition had the advantage that

> if a speaker's words did not come through because he had turned away from the mounted microphone, we would merely move a phone off one ear and catch his voice coming over our glass partition.[15]

Elisabeth Heyward, interpreter at the trial and later at the UN, found that the equipment and the sound insulation in Nuremberg were rudimentary. Booths were not soundproof, and interpreters could hear other languages.[16] This must have been especially troublesome when the interpreter nicknamed the "Passionate Haystack" was working in the courtroom.[17] She "produced the most inescapable and nerve-wracking sound—a penetrating twang which provided a steady background screech on many of the sound recordings of the trial."[18]

The Electrical Transmission System

The communication in the courtroom was made possible by a wired system consisting of microphones, cables, amplifiers and headphones. There were various microphones in the courtroom. One microphone was placed at the rostrum from which both defense and prosecution spoke, one at the witness box; four microphones were placed on the Bench in front of the judges, although only one at a time could be active. Four more microphones were at the interpreters' desks, two in the front row and two in the back row. Finally, one portable microphone was installed for the use of the marshal of the court, and it was occasionally put by a guard in front of the defendants' dock for their use. The microphones on the bench and at the interpreters' desks had an on-off switch.

From any microphone except the interpreters',

the voice is carried to an RCA 76-B console and RCA QP-7 portable mixer. From the RCA mixer, the verbatim speech picked up from any one of [these] microphones is relayed on Channel Number 1 to the IBM amplifiers. From there they are relayed to the interpreting tables. The interpreter's translation into his microphone is then relayed on the designated channel, via the IBM amplifiers to the audience.[19]

Microphones and headphones were connected through electrical, "telephonic wires."[20]

At every place where a microphone was installed, one or more sets of headphones were present for the use of the speaker.[21] Headsets were available at every chair, too. There were some 600 headsets with selector switch in the courtroom. They were "US Army Signal Corps headsets, with two metal bands on top of the head connecting the large earphones on either side."[22] The switch was located either on the table or on "the armrests of the seats in the press and visitors' gallery."[23] For chairs without arms, it was connected to the headphones with a cable and was held by the listener or left loose on the floor.

Not everyone was comfortable with the use of microphones. The judges sometimes forgot to switch off their microphones, so that confidential conversations could be overheard through the headphones.[24] Lawyers had to abandon the habit of interrupting each other and had to learn to wait for their turn. As Jackson pointed out from the very beginning, "the prosecution will have to arrange its case in such a manner that only one man will be trying to use the prosecution microphone at one time. They can't all talk at once."[25]

In order to control access to the microphones, a sound monitor was placed at the back of the courtroom. This technician sat behind a glass cage near the press gallery and was responsible for the on-off switch of the microphones. It was necessary to keep the number of open microphones to a minimum in order to avoid excessive noise[26] and "the screech of 'feedback.'"[27]

> [The technician] had to be constantly on the alert, very quick in the uptake, and possess the finger technique of a pianist. His principle [sic] source of anxiety was the Bench, any one of whose members was liable to address the court without warning.[28]

The sound monitor also controlled the volume level. Some speakers used a softer tone of voice than others, or spoke closer to the microphone, and it was crucial for the interpreters to be able to hear clearly at any time.[29]

There was a second sound control room, a small, "mysterious"[30] room to the right of the German desk (called "sound control room" in the plan of the courtroom, Fig. IV). In this room, connected to the courtroom through a doorway, an American military technician controlled the amplifiers for each of the five channels. Here Army Signal Corps under Major Vincent operated the wire recorders used for the phonographic record of the trial. The technicians in this room were also responsible for the frequent technical problems that afflicted the electrical system, which amounted to "four tons of various electrical gadgets."[31]

Unlike today's interpreting systems, in which the voice is transmitted via radio, the Nuremberg system consisted of cables that lay uncovered on the floor. The *Justizpalast* in Nuremberg was not a frame building; it was built in solid masonry and for this reason it was not possible to lay the cables of the interpreting system under the floor. People often stumbled on them and disconnected them, thus plunging the system into silence. Sessions had to be interrupted, sometimes for hours, until Major Vincent's technicians had found the hitches and repaired them. Eventually, planks of wood were installed to protect the cables. It also happened that during quick repairs the wires were crossed and produced the wrong translation. People dialing French would hear the German translation, for example. Finally, old wire insulation was responsible for a problem called "cross-talk": people selecting one language would actually hear two, and both unintelligible:

> Soudain l'avocat disait: "Votre Honneur, la traduction n'est pas claire. J'entends deux voix en même temps; il y a l'allemand et le français."

> Le Président suspendait la séance, et les techniciens s'affairaient autour des fils.[32]

This hitch, too, required long suspensions of the sessions because "cross-talk" was hard to spot and repair.

Team System

Even more interesting than the technical aspects of the interpreting system was the organization of work at the interpreters' desks. A complicated pattern of personnel rotation had been devised for the Nuremberg courtroom. There were 36 interpreters who alternated at the microphone according to their assigned language, so that no interpreter would be required to work longer than was considered feasible.

As mentioned, four groups of three interpreters were present in the courtroom at any time. These four desks, a total of 12 interpreters, constituted a team. There were two other teams of 12 interpreters. As Alfred Steer, Head of the Translation Division, describes:

> we fielded three complete teams of twelve interpreters each, as follows:
>
> Team I—on duty
>
> Team II—on stand-by in a room nearby, listening to the proceedings in the court room, each interpreter ready at a moment's notice to be substituted in case his equivalent in the court room should falter.
>
> Team III—at liberty, resting up.[33]

Teams I and II. The three teams of 12 interpreters alternated in such a way that each team would only work two days out of three. Still, it was noticed that a single interpreter could not be on duty the whole day, from 10 a.m. to 5 p.m. when the court was in session.[34] Therefore, while one team had the day off, the other two teams alternated at the microphone according to the following schedule:

	Team I	Team II
10:00 a.m. to 11:25 a.m.	on duty	on reserve
mid-morning recess		
11:35 a.m. to 1:00 p.m.	on reserve	on duty
noon recess		
2:00 p.m. to 3:25 p.m.	on reserve	on duty
mid-afternoon recess		
3:35 p.m. to 5:00 p.m.	on duty	on reserve

Interpreters worked shifts of 85 minutes, i.e., roughly three hours a day on two days out of three. The shifts were longer than today's shifts of 30 minutes but, as a whole, for one day "the working schedule for the interpreters [at Nuremberg] provided for fewer hours in the booth than does the charter for Permanent Interpreters today,"[35] who according to the AIIC contract, usually work two and a half to three hours in the morning and two and a half to three hours in the afternoon.[36] At the IMT trial it was noticed that if the interpreters were kept longer on the microphone, the quality of their interpreting would fall.

The interpreters on standby listened to the proceedings in a back room through earphones connected to a special channel. At the beginning, the backup interpreters had no opportunity to hear the proceedings and they complained that they did not know what was going on in the trial when they were called on duty.[37] It was crucial for them to know the topic of discussion as specifically as possible, so that they could anticipate what they would be interpreting and prepare themselves through the use of dictionaries and glossaries. Later on, earphones for the second team were installed in the standby room. This also ensured a degree of continuity and standard vocabulary, because the interpreters conformed to the version that had been used so far by their colleagues.

Team III.   As for the third team, at the beginning of the trial they had their day off. Interpreters were working two days and resting up the third, and how they spent their time was up to them. Later on in the trial, this arrangement was changed so that day-off meant off court, but not at rest: interpreters spent the third day checking the transcripts of their translation against the verbatim recording. It was basically an off-court day providing welcome relief from the strain of courtroom interpreting; but it was spent in activities related to their job.[38] Some interpreters of the third team were involved in the translation of documents that were soon going to be used in court or in other linguistic tasks aimed at improving their performance as interpreters. Others worked at the private hearings of the judges, who often met after sessions to discuss the day's proceedings. Most interpreters had additional duties. "Between sessions they were assigned to other departments, like investigations, translation, transcript correction... the idea that they would do nothing was not established."[39] Sometimes interpreters would work for the prosecution as investigators. They were sent to countries in Europe to obtain affidavits from potential witnesses and their agreement to testify personally in court.

Why did the interpreters need three teams? This seems to have been a frequently asked question at the time, since Mr. Uiberall reports that they "had to fight for the third team."[40] The officers in charge of hiring personnel probably thought that it was a waste of money, and that there was no need to have two teams in court and an extra team off duty. There are many reasons why this was not the case, according to those involved.

The second team on standby was necessary because the nature of the job required that people not work behind the microphones for a whole day. The job was described as "nerve-racking,"[41] as it required an extraordinary capacity for concentration even in stressful situations; the subject matter of testimony was often such that it provoked an additional emotional strain for the interpreters. Working conditions were also uncomfortable, because of the small, hot booths and because of the necessity for interpreters to speak softly. Moreover, as Léon Dostert points out, "rotation of personnel... took care of unavoidable absence from duty":[42] a complete team of 12 interpreters had to be present in the courtroom at any time; to avoid the risk of having to stop the proceedings because of a missing interpreter, a replacement had to be available at any given moment. Finally, a replacement was sometimes needed because an interpreter would break down and was not able to continue. For all these reasons, the two teams alternated during the day. Still, teams I and II were constantly under strain, either because they were on duty or because they were listening to the proceedings and had to be ready to step in at any time. They needed a day off-court to recover from the strain. This is why the third team was necessary.

The Translation Division soon realized that the system of rotation among the three teams was in fact necessary to ensure more accuracy in translation. Not only were the interpreters able to physically rest from the mental strain of interpreting. During their day off they could also check on their work and see how it could be improved. They could look up words and expressions and ask for clarifications. They worked as editors and translators, thus becoming more familiar with the vocabulary. Hence, though at first it seemed to be a waste of money and a sign of laziness on the part of interpreters, the team system turned out to be a crucial aspect of interpretation.

Language Policy.   According to the language policy adopted at Nuremberg, interpreters would translate only into one language and there would be no relay system. A different policy would have interpreters translate back and forth between two languages. An interpreter working from French into German also translates German into French. This policy would have reduced the number of interpreters needed at the Nuremberg Trial, as shown by the following figure (each line represents one interpreter):

Figure V

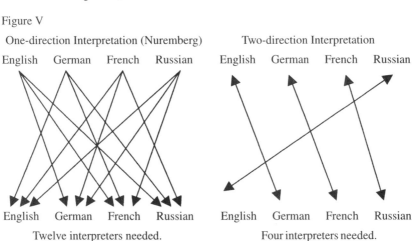

One-direction Interpretation (Nuremberg)   Two-direction Interpretation

English   German   French   Russian   English   German   French   Russian

English   German   French   Russian   English   German   French   Russian

Twelve interpreters needed.   Four interpreters needed.

In the early stages of the trial organization, Charles Horsky, of the U.S. Office Chief of Counsel, reported to Justice Jackson that the number of interpreters needed would vary according to their ability to translate in both directions. Horsky was not knowledgeable about interpretation, but had been surprised to find out that there were people who were able to translate *from* a language but not *into* that language.[43] But at the trial it was noticed that interpreters, with a few exceptions, are more fluent in one language than in others they work with, and therefore they work at best only into one language. Moreover, two-direction interpretation would also have put twice as much pressure on the interpreters. Thus it was decided that the policy of back-and-forth interpreting should not be adopted: at Nuremberg, every interpreter translated only in one direction. If they interpreted Russian into English, they would not interpret English into Russian during the same session.

Nuremberg also did not feature a relay system. In a relay system, when more than two languages are used in a conference, interpreting is done directly into only one language, for example, English. The interpreters translating into the other languages pick up from the English translation and reinterpret into the language to which they are assigned. This mode requires half the interpreting personnel compared to a non-relay system. At Nuremberg, for example, a relay system would have required six interpreters instead of 12 . (See Figure VI: every line represents one interpreter.) If English is chosen as the "intermediary" language, for example, and English is spoken at the moment, the three translators into Russian, French and German pick up from the verbatim. If German is spoken, the German-English translator gives a version that is used by the French and Russian interpreters to retranslate into their languages.[44]

Figure VI

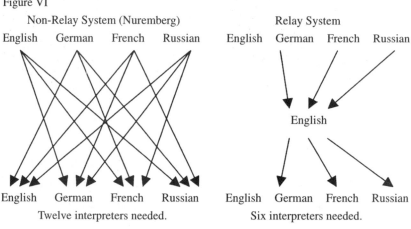

Non-Relay System (Nuremberg)   Relay System

English   German   French   Russian   English   German   French   Russian

English   German   French   Russian   English   German   French   Russian
    Twelve interpreters needed.   Six interpreters needed.

The disadvantages of relay, however, made it unsuitable for the Nuremberg Trial. First, the loss of accuracy can be remarkable because of the double translation involved; second, there is a considerable delay between the original and the interpreted versions. This would have been a major disadvantage at the trial, where the defense and the prosecution had to hear what was said quickly enough to raise objections in time.

Yet, in the early stages of the planning of the trial, the system was devised to include relay. Charles Horsky informed Justice Jackson that it would not be possible to find a translator into French, for example, who could understand all three other languages. Thus the interpreter, it was thought, would have to wait for a translation into a language he or she knew, such as English, and reinterpret that into French. Horsky suggested that the "middle" language be English, considering that two fifths of the trial would be carried out in that language. When I asked Peter Uiberall, interpreter at Nuremberg, if the idea of a relay system had ever been taken into consideration, he answered that

> Yes, somebody suggested that, as a presumably money-saving arrange-
> ment. But the idea was quickly dropped, as it would have wasted in
> time what might have been saved on personnel. Most important, this
> "subsequent simultaneous" interpretation would surely... be less accu-
> rate, and that was a risk no one would seriously want to take in these
> highly critical, criminal proceedings.[45]

Figure VII—Monitoring the interpretation. Capt. Harry Sperber, who usually translates German into English, monitors the interpretation.

Source: National Archives, College Park, MD.

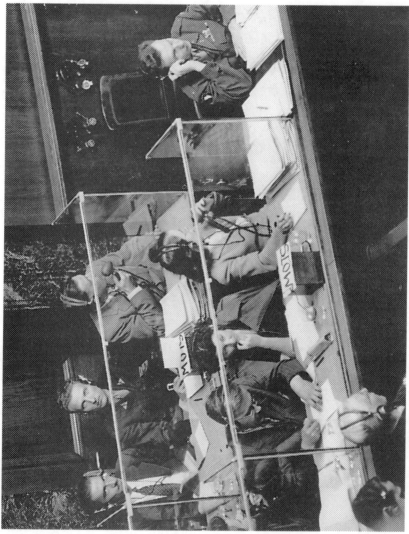

Figure VIII—Interpreters during a session of the IMT. Front: the English desk; back: the German desk. To the right, Lt. Walter Selogson, monitor. Note that German is spoken because the English, French and Russian desks are active; the three interpreters turn to their left to see the speaker at the witness stand.

Source: National Archives, College Park, MD.

The relay system was used in case of emergencies. The text "Information Concerning Interpreters" reports of a case in which

> the Russian-German interpreter was seized with an uncontrollable fit of coughing during a Russian speech, so his colleague who was responsible for English-German switched his earphones to the English channel and reinterpreted the English interpretation into German for a few minutes until the coughing interpreter's relief could take his seat. This shift was accomplished without break and without even the knowledge of more than one or two people in the courtroom.[46]

The Monitor

Already during the mock trials, it was discovered that the interpreting system needed someone to supervise its smooth functioning. This person could not be one of the interpreters, because they completely devoted their attention to translating. It was decided that a monitor would be present at all times in court. He would supervise interpreters, and he would also facilitate their task by reminding the tribunal to speak at the proper pace.

The monitor was a member of the Translation Division, usually an officer, sitting between the English desk and the marshal of the court (see Figures VII and VIII). He was responsible for monitoring the accuracy of the interpretation and the functioning of the equipment, and for the communication between interpreters and the court.

First of all, the monitor was assigned a team of interpreters and he was responsible for having the whole team present and ready for each session, both every morning and after recesses. In the courtroom, in order to check on the interpretation and its accuracy, the monitor wore two split earphones and listened to the verbatim and to the various channels. He was thus able, for example, to signal to a desk that their microphone was erroneously off or to an interpreter that he was speaking too loud, disturbing his or her colleagues.

The monitor also made sure that the interpreters received the speaker's voice clearly. At his position he had a telephone connection with the sound technician at the back of the room. The telephone had a light instead of a bell, so that it would not disturb the proceedings. The monitor would tell the technician to regulate the volume of the verbatim that was coming through to the interpreters and the volume of the translation going to the listeners. Speakers and interpreters spoke at different distances from the microphones and with different volumes. It was necessary to keep the outgoing volume constant, otherwise it might be tiring for the listeners.[47] If the sound technician could not help, the monitor would step in personally. For example, he would put the microphone closer to the speaker at the witness stand.[48]

Another function of the monitor was to procure documents for the interpreters. This involved obtaining prepared speeches by defense or prosecution, but in particular it meant that the monitor asked in advance which evidentiary documents were going to be read by defense or prosecution. Since the documents read in court were often translations, the monitor provided interpreters with the original text in order to avoid the inaccuracy and confusion of double translation.

By far the most important function of the monitor was to ensure the accuracy of translation, which he did by operating the yellow and red light system. This system had been devised during the initial mock trials. It was basically a system of silent communication between the monitor, acting on behalf of interpreters, and the speakers, in which the former informed the latter of the necessity of changing the pace of the speech. The light system allowed him to cope with technical hitches in the equipment, but especially with the considerable "human" problems affecting interpreters, as explained below. Red and yellow bulbs were placed from the start in front of Presiding Judge Lawrence; later on they were also installed at the speaker's rostrum and at the witness stand.

The Yellow Light.   The switches for the yellow and red lights were at the monitor's position. If the monitor thought that speed of delivery was too high and the translation inadequate, he flashed the yellow light, and the speaker was required to speak more slowly. Interpreters had found out during mock trials that there was a certain speed beyond which simultaneous interpreting was impossible. Speakers tended to speak very quickly when reading from written texts, preventing the interpreter from delivering an accurate translation, especially the texts had not been made available to the interpreters.[49] The yellow light also indicated the need for pauses between questions and answers, in order to allow interpreters to finish their translations and pass the microphone to the appropriate interpreter. Some texts report that the trial sometimes proceeded at dictation speed, sixty words per minute,[50] while the average interpreting speed was 130 words, with peaks of 200.[51] It was discovered that, for beginning interpreters, the average speed at which they could perform well was 100 words per minute and for excellent well-trained people, 150 was not excessive. Translated into pages, this meant that interpreters were able to translate 15 double-spaced legal-sized pages per hour;[52] with the pre-translated text the translation could be synchronized even more with the original text and carried out at the pace of 30 pages per hour.[53]

The tribunal often warned speakers not to exceed a reasonable and feasible pace of speech, as Presiding Judge Lawrence did with a witness:

> Answer slowly and after pausing. Do you understand?... Wait a minute, wait a minute. When you see the light on the desk there or here it means you are going too fast. Do you understand?[54]

On another occasion, January 31, 1946, the defense lawyers complained that they were getting a wrong interpretation of the French original. The numbers in particular were often mistranslated. It was important for them to get the correct page number that the French prosecutor was quoting from the document book, so that they could find the documents to which he referred. Once again, Lawrence intervened to solve the problem. He addressed the French Prosecutor Dubost:

> Mr. Dubost, I think the trouble really arises from the fact that you give the numbers too fast and the numbers are very often wrongly translated not only into German, but sometimes into English. It is very difficult for the interpreters to pick up all these numbers. First of all you are giving the numbers of the document, then the number of the exhibit, then the page of the document book—and that means that the interpreters have got to translate many numbers spoken very quickly... and therefore it is absolutely essential that you go slowly.[55]

But with certain speakers not even warnings or the light system worked, and the interpreters had to resort to other means:

> By nature Jackson spoke quickly... He kept a note [the interpreters] once sent him on a torn scrap of tissue paper: Will you please tell the Justice that we will break down if he does not slow down.[56]

For such cases, when the speakers did not cooperate with interpreters by minding the yellow light, the red light signal was devised, which required the speaker to stop altogether.

The Red Light.   The red light was used to signal a number of problems requiring the interruption of the proceedings. At times, when the monitor flashed the red light, this meant that the interpreter had not been able to hear or understand the last few sentences and the speaker was required to stop and repeat. If the red light was flashed for a longer time, it meant that the interpreter was not able to continue her or his translation, because of a coughing spell, for example. In this case, the speaker had to stop until the light was turned off. Finally, the monitor might punch the red light to stop the entire proceedings for a short time, like a couple of minutes, in order to allow the interpreter to regain composure and be ready to continue.

The monitor could also require a longer interruption when he deemed that an interpreter would not be able to continue and needed to be replaced. He had a telephone connection also to the nearby room, where the second team of interpreters were in reserve, and would use it to call in interpreters to substitute their equivalent in the courtroom. The reserve interpreters usually knew when they were going to be called in because they could hear their colleagues on duty getting slower and less accurate. Finally, the monitor requested adjournments when the system needed repair. If a long interruption was requested, Judge Lawrence, whenever possible, called for a recess, in order to minimize the loss of time. A short recess was scheduled in the morning and in the afternoon, and a longer recess was taken around 1:00 p.m. for lunch.

Replacements.   The monitor sometimes needed to replace even the best interpreters because of the very nature of the material to be interpreted. It happened sometimes that an interpreter would falter because of the emotional strain connected to the nature of testimony. It is reported that some interpreters would freeze because of a shock effect in reaction to testimony regarding massacres and concentration camps. Others report of young and inexperienced interpreters breaking down and crying, or being unable to start at all. A replacement could also take place because interpreters themselves asked to be taken out. The following description by John Dos Passos shows to what point the interpreters were affected by what they were translating:

> When the prosecutor reaches the crimes against the Jews [the defendants] freeze into an agony of attention. The voice of the German translator follows the prosecutor's voice like a shrill echo of vengeance. Through the glass partition beside the prisoners' box you can see the taut face between gleaming earphones of the dark-haired woman who is making the translation. There is a look of horror on her face. Sometimes her throat seems to stiffen so that she can hardly speak the terrible words. They are cringing now... [Jackson's] voice is that of a reasonable man appalled by the crimes he has discovered, but echoing it is the choked, sterile German of the woman interpreter that hovers over the prisoners' box like a gadfly.[57]

Some of the interpreters had been in concentration camps and were considered the best personnel to interpret the material regarding the camps, but it was hard for them to be brought back to those experiences. On those occasions, interpreters were required to hide or overcome the resentment they felt against the defendants. They had to make an effort to be calm and fair to them in their translation.[58]

For example, a new recruit, a girl of Jewish background who performed well during the training program, froze and started to cry the first time she was on duty in the courtroom. She could not overcome the thought that: "Because of those men, twelve of the fourteen men in my family are dead."[59] On another occasion, the interpreter could not continue the job, not because he was a victim, but because of the sense of guilt of being the aggressor.

> [He was] an interpreter who had been a lieutenant in the German armed forces. One day he came into the office in tears. I [Uiberall] said, "What's wrong?" And he said, "I cannot go on. They are talking about the Warsaw ghetto, the uprising, the massacre. I was one of the German troops who had to do this. I just can't go on." He was released from his assignment with the interpreting branch, but was later picked up by the German defense, and he worked for them as a linguist.[60]

Sometimes the shock effect was delayed, and the interpreters only realized the full meaning of testimony during the night. Many reported they had nightmares, for example, about the horrors of the films that the U.S. Army had taken when they first entered the concentration camps.[61] Interpreters were forced to see these movies because they were required to interpret them as they were shown. It is reported that Judge Parker had to stay in bed "for three days after seeing in court the Russian film on atrocities in Eastern Europe."[62]

Qualities of a Monitor.   In order to carry out all the duties mentioned above, the monitor had to be very knowledgeable about the simultaneous system of interpretation and particularly sensitive to signs of weakness on the part of interpreters. He was required to understand most of the working languages of the court. In his text of 1946, Alfred Steer, monitor and Head of the Translation Division, points out the characteristics of a good monitor:

> A sense of responsibility, ability to handle people, initiative to see what is necessary and to get it done, and a personality adequate to deal in liaison fashion with all participants in the trial from the judges to the defendants is necessary. Of particular importance for the monitor is the ability to remain calm under pressure. Equipment occasionally fails, interpreters become excited, speakers are slow in cooperating, etc. In all these cases, the monitor is the man responsible for putting things right.[63]

Peter Uiberall acted as a monitor on several occasions. Beside checking that the translation was accurate, he would listen to the rhythm of translation and the breathing of the interpreter. Usually, when an interpreter started to slow down and breathe hard, it was a clear sign that he or she was running out of energy and was soon going to break down. He would punch the yellow light asking for slower speech, if he thought that this would be enough to help the failing interpreter, or he would flash the red light and ask for a few minutes interruption in order to find a substitute for the interpreter. Sometimes, Mr. Uiberall reports, if the interpreter in trouble was the German into English interpreter sitting next to him, he would take the microphone and translate until the interpreter was able to continue on his or her own.[64]

Alfred Steer, when acting as a monitor, paid attention to the *décalage*, that is, the lag between the original and interpreted versions. He considered a lag of eight to 10 seconds normal. If interpreters lagged behind more than that, he knew he would have to substitute them soon. With this strategy, he says, he could check on languages he did not know very well, such as Russian:

> My Russian was never very good, but I would take a split set of head-phones, listening to the Russian in one ear and the original in the other ear, and I would listen for the cognates. For instance, their word for "tribunal" is "tribunaliye." So if I didn't get it within about eight seconds, that interpreter had to be replaced.[65]

Interpreting as done at Nuremberg was totally new, and the Translation Division had to devise solutions that were appropriate to the needs of the trial and that ensured its smooth functioning. Some of these solutions are still known today. The yellow light, for example, connected to a "slow" button in the booth survives still today. Unfortunately for interpreters, however, today's speakers have long learned to ignore the light and there is no monitor to warn them to "look for the light."

Other Features of the Interpreting System

The need for linguistic services at Nuremberg did not just amount to the need for communication between the bench and the witness stand, though this was the most important segment of the communication in the courtroom. In addition to simultaneous extempore interpretation, the system included bench interpreting, interpreting of languages other than the official working languages and the combination of written and oral translation.

Judges' Interpreters.   The service of interpretation for the judges included bench interpreting and interpretation in the consultation room. Most of the judges, in fact, could speak one or two foreign languages, but not accurately enough to know the legal terminology in those languages. The French Judge Donnedieu de Vabres "was familiar with German, but knew only three or four words of English, usually out of context, which on occasion he liked to exercise."[66] Biddle, the American Member, could speak French and understood German, and made himself the fulcrum of Western delegations.[67] "Volchov [the Russian Alternate Member] could carry out a limited conversation in English—he had lived in London for several years."[68] He had been working for the Soviet Foreign Ministry and sent to London to the Soviet embassy.[69] The Russian Judge Nikitchenko could understand and speak English perfectly, but he steadfastly refused to acknowledge it. He and Volchov would only talk through their interpreters. Only occasionally would they enjoy surprising their British and American colleagues with witty remarks in English.[70]

Thus the judges needed interpreters both inside and outside the courtroom. Inside the courtroom, their questions and comments were generally translated over the interpreting system. However, they sometimes made remarks to each other or asked each other questions that were not to be heard by the whole courtroom, and therefore could not be translated through the interpreting system. For this reason, two bench interpreters were present in the courtroom at any time. The interpreters serving as bench interpreters were Oleg Troyanovsky and Benjamin Wald, both at least trilingual.[71]

The two bench interpreters sat behind the judges, one between the Russian and British delegations, and one between the American and French judges. On November 13, 1945, during one of the dress rehearsals, Francis Biddle had arranged the seating of the judges in such a way as to minimize the number of bench interpreters. The American and British delegations sat in the middle. The French sat to the left of the Americans and the Russians to the right of the Englishmen. "Everyone accepted this scheme as logical, since it placed the four English-speaking judges together."[72]

The judges resorted to the bench interpreters for their consultations during court sessions or recesses, and also in particular instances. In the first "incident" of the trial,[73] for example, a former Nazi General, von dem Bach-Zelewski, testified against the defendants. When he passed in front of the defendants' dock to leave the room, Göring rose and called him "*Schweinehund!*"[74] loud enough for the whole court to hear. The interpreters in the booths did not translate the insult, since it did not come to them through the headphones, and the judges leaned back towards the bench interpreters to inquire about its meaning.[75]

Outside the courtroom, the judges needed interpreters for their deliberations. At the beginning of the trial, when the judges met in closed sessions to discuss prosecution or defense requests, consecutive interpreting was used. Subsequently it was thought that the simultaneous interpreting system might be adapted to fit the judges' consultation room. Around December 12, 1945, the simultaneous interpreting system was also installed in this room. Biddle, the American judge, wrote in his notes: "The earphones are now installed in our consultation room, and works [sic] well, saving time."[76]

The room consisted of a long table with six microphones where the judges sat with their assistants. Each chair had earphones and a switch. The languages used were only three, English, Russian and French, and consequently there were three interpreting booths in three corners of the room. Only two interpreters sat at each table, which was furnished with a glass panel to avoid interference from their voices. The best and most discreet interpreters were chosen for the job, and the system worked well. The judges were able to discuss and argue as if they had been speaking the same language.[77] Interpreting for the judges was more difficult than in the courtroom, because it was impossible to impose the same discipline on them as on the speakers in the courtroom. They would speak fast and not wait for their turn. There were no yellow or red lights to slow them down or stop them, and no monitor to help the interpreters. This is why only the best interpreters were selected, and they worked without supervision.[78]

The need for interpreters for the judges was present not only inside the courthouse, but whenever the judges needed to speak to each other. This was the case in the corridors during recesses, as well as at parties and dinners organized by and for the judges and other court members. The American Judge Biddle remembers a dinner party held by the Russian Judge Nikitchenko. Nikitchenko had a "pretty, gentle secretary-interpreter, Miss Ninna Orlova," who translated for him though he could speak and understand English.[79] More importantly, interpreters were needed during the deliberation on sentences. On that occasion the interpreters lived in with the judges and could not leave the premises at any time throughout the deliberations; they were not allowed to communicate with the outside world, for obvious security reasons.[80]

Interpreters for "Minor" Languages.   Another special need of the Nuremberg Trial was interpretation for "minor" languages, that is, languages that were used only occasionally and therefore did not have their own "booth."

On a few occasions, witnesses were called who did not speak any of the four working languages of the tribunal. For these instances "special" interpreters were hired, and they sat next to the witness in the witness box. If the French prosecution team had called the witness, then the "special" interpreter would translate into French. If he or she was a witness for the Russian prosecution, then the translation at the witness stand would be from and into Russian. It was the interpreter at the witness stand who spoke into the microphone instead of the witness. As soon as the question was asked by counsel or by the prosecution, the interpreter would whisper the translation in the witness's ear. In the meantime, the question was translated into the three other court languages by the regular interpreting crew. The witness replied to the interpreter who translated the answer into the microphone. The interpreters for the other languages picked up from this translation. The interpreter at the witness stand did not necessarily need to wear the headphones, but questions from the bench or the defense in a language he or she did not know were always possible.

This technique was used for a Belgian witness called to testify about the university library collection of her town, which had been stolen by the Nazis.[81] On a different occasion, the Russian prosecution called a Polish witness and the tribunal hired a Polish-Russian interpreter for the job. Other languages occasionally used were Bulgarian, Czech, Hungarian and Yiddish. This method was fairly efficient and showed the flexibility of the simultaneous interpreting system. It had two major disadvantages, though. First, it was a relay system, and as such it involved a double translation, with possible loss of accuracy. Second, the only recorded version was the version given by the interpreter at the witness stand. The original version as given by the witness was not officially recorded and there was no way to check the accuracy of the translation, or to have the exact verbatim version for future reference.[82] Yet the tribunal had to put up with the inconvenience because there was no other feasible alternative to this system, and it was considered adequate enough to meet the accuracy standards of the tribunal.

Combinations of Oral and Written Translations.   Interpreting as performed at Nuremberg did not involve only simultaneous translation as it has been described so far. Depending on the availability of the written copy of the speeches to be made in the courtroom, a number of other interpreting techniques could be adopted, such as reading of pretranslated speeches and sight translations. These techniques required the cooperation of the speakers if they were to ensure smooth communication within the tribunal. However, this was often not the case in Nuremberg.

The reading of pretranslated speeches was performed when the prosecution or the defense read prepared speeches or written documents in court, and gave the texts to the interpreters well beforehand; the interpreters translated the speeches before the court session and read the translation simultaneously with the original version. When this happened, as for the prosecutors' opening speeches, the translation could be perfectly synchronized with the original speech. The interpreters reading the translations only had to look for last-minute changes and translate them extemporaneously.

Sight translation was used when the speakers used prepared speeches, but they gave them to the interpreters too late for them to translate before the court session. When this happened, interpreters would normally have the text in front of their eyes in the booth and translate by reading from it. In this case, too, they had to pay attention to unexpected changes in the original version. Because of the difficulty of reading while paying attention to the original speech to make sure that it corresponded to the text, some interpreters preferred to abandon the written text altogether and interpret simultaneously only what came through the earphones.

However, because of the nature of the trial, prepared speeches were not frequent. Court members usually delivered impromptu speeches and remarks, and these had to be translated extempore by the interpreters. Speakers sometimes informed the interpreters through briefings about the nature of their speech. This helped the interpreters prepare for the kind of speech they would have to translate, and they could also review or learn the vocabulary relevant to the subject.

By far the most difficult situation for interpreters occurred when the speakers read from texts they had not made available to the interpreters. Orators generally read faster than they spoke, putting the interpreters under considerable pressure. Moreover, the lack of texts for the interpreters was the cause of two major problems that were long debated and that slowed down the proceedings. First of all, the availability of texts for the interpreters was particularly important when evidentiary documents were read out in court. During examination, for example, an American prosecutor would read out the English version of a captured German document and then ask the defendant to acknowledge the authorship of the document. In these instances, the into-German interpreter definitely needed to have the original German text in front of his or her eyes. In this way the inaccuracies of the double translation would be avoided and, more important, the defendant could be tied down to specific sentences in the document. Otherwise, a defendant could not be asked to recognize his words after a double translation.

Thus, before each session, the monitor would go to the speakers and ask them which documents they would be reading out loud, and ask for original copies. Judge Francis Biddle, too, was well aware of this necessity, as he pointed out at one of the International Military Tribunal's Executive Sessions:

> Mr. Biddle suggested that a photostat copy of each document be given to the German interpreter prior to its presentation in court in order that the relevant portions might be read into the microphone directly from the text.[83]

Biddle also wrote in his notes that his suggestion had been adopted:

> A captured document in OKW (High Command) files—PS 789, Ex. 23, offered—German original text is handed interpreter—Reads portion marked.[84]

However, although everyone agreed on the necessity to provide interpreters with the original document text, interpreters only seldom received the texts that were going to be read. This problem, for example, affected the defendant Hans Fritzsche, who reports it in his memoirs:

> For the whole of my defense I had to make do with a few extracts from my talks which the British radio had, on one occasion, made use of for its own purposes. These had been translated into English and were now retranslated into German. The double translation had so distorted the sense of many words they had become unrecognizable.[85]

This was probably the major shortcoming of the interpreting system in Nuremberg, as explained later on. Paradoxically, during his cross-examination, Hermann Göring was given the original German texts of the evidence presented against him, but these texts were not given to the interpreters. Thus he did not miss the chance to point out several times that what he heard through the earphones were not his exact words, and that his meaning had changed due to the double translation.

The other major problem about documents was that, at the beginning, the Translating Branch could not keep up with the enormous amount of translation they were required to perform. This created many difficulties for the prosecutors, because all the documents presented in court were supposed to be translated beforehand into the three other languages and made available to all court members. Often, a prosecutor started his case based on an English copy of a document. Upon inquiry of the bench, it was soon discovered that the translations were not available, and the case had to be postponed.

In order to solve this problem, the tribunal ruled that the relevant portions of evidence be read in court so that they would be translated simultaneously. The translations would then be transcribed by the court reporters and be available to the members of the tribunal by the end of the day.[86] The interpreters had to face the paradox that, instead of being able to read from translations that should have been made beforehand, they had to interpret documents simultaneously, in order to provide those translations that had not been made. Speakers would read the documents quickly, because they wanted to proceed with their case, and the interpreters often could not cope with the pace. Thus, the accuracy of the translation was probably lower than usual, but this only happened at the beginning of the trial.[87]

The issues of the availability of written translations and the permission to read out evidence in court were discussed over and over in numerous sessions. It is the only issue about translation that created resentment and the feeling of being wronged among both defense and prosecution. It was mainly a failure of the Translating Branch, which could not cope with the amount of translations to be done because it was understaffed. This problem affected the Interpreting Branch, too, as I mentioned, but it was not a shortcoming of the interpreting system. On the contrary, the interpreting system and all its related systems seemed to work fairly well. As speakers delivered their speeches, translations would come through the earphones. And yet, how could everyone in the courtroom be sure that what they heard was an accurate and faithful translation of the original words? How could they trust interpreting? And also, what was the impact of interpreting on the trial? These issues went beyond the practical organization of microphones and cable connections. Issues such as the reliability of the system and the impact of interpretation could not be tackled *a priori*. They had to be dealt with during the course of the trial. These issues are discussed in the next chapter.

Notes

1. Ann and John Tusa, *The Nuremberg Trial* (London: Macmillan, 1983): 218.
2. Maurice Bardèche, *Nuremberg ou la terre promise* (Paris: Les Sept Couleurs, 1948): 29. "What struck people's imaginations most." My translation.
3. *Stars and Stripes* (Nov. 20, 1945), qtd. in Ann and John Tusa, *The Nuremberg Trial* (London: Macmillan, 1983): 147. See Fig. I for a picture of the courtroom.
4. Rolf Schneider, *Prozeß in Nürnberg* (Frankfurt am Mein: Fischer, 1968): foreword. "On November 14 [sic], 1945 in Nuremberg began the trial against the major German war criminals before an International Military Tribunal. The number of defendants: 21, of judges: 8, of prosecutors: 50, of witnesses: 111, of defense counsel: 23. It was carried out in four languages simultaneously. The trial lasted one year." My translation.
5. David Maxwell-Fyfe Kilmuir, *Political Adventure: The Memoirs of the Earl of Kilmuir* (London: Weidenfeld, 1964): 97.

6. The verbatim is always original, regardless of language; it is therefore made up of speeches in different languages, except for languages other than the official languages, as explained in chapter 2 "Interpreters for Minor Languages."

7. Evidence of this problem can be seen in the excerpts of the videorecording of the Nuremberg Trial (AIIC, *Nurnberg*, Geneva 1992, videocassette). Dostert is monitoring the interpretation and listens to the French channel. Suddenly he turns to the French desk and signals to them that no translation is coming through. The interpreters at the desk quickly turn on the microphone.

8. It was the duty of the monitor to prevent this from happening, as explained below.

9. The technique of passing the microphone can be seen in the video excerpts of the Nuremberg trial (AIIC, *Nurnberg*, Geneva 1992, videocassette). Interpreters sit very close, almost hugging, and sometimes keep the microphone between the two interpreters involved, so that they can both speak into it without moving it.

10. E. Peter Uiberall, "Court Interpreting at the Nuremberg Trial" (ts. April 11, 1995): 3. The sketch is to be read as follows: E = English, F = French, G = German and R = Russian.

11. E. Peter Uiberall, "Court Interpreting at the Nuremberg Trial" (ts. April 11, 1995): 3.

12. Marie-France Skuncke, AIIC, *The Interpreters: A Historical Perspective*, videocassette.

13. For a comment on the relationship and cooperation between interpreters and defendants see chapter 3 "Reliability and Impact of the Interpretation."

14. Conference (AIIC, *Nurnberg*, Geneva 1992, videocassette). "We had to eat the microphone in order not to disturb the others. We had to speak with the mike in the mouth." My translation.

15. E. Peter Uiberall, letter to the author (Feb. 11, 1995).

16. Interview (AIIC, *Nurnberg*, Geneva 1992, videocassette).

17. See biographical information on Margot Bortlin in the chapter 5 "Profiles of Interpreters" and her picture on the cover of the book.

18. Ann and John Tusa, *The Nuremberg Trial* (London: Macmillan, 1983): 218.

19. Léon Dostert, "The Instantaneous Multi-Lingual Interpreting System in the International Military Tribunal" (ts. n.d.): 3.

20. Whitney R. Harris, *Tyranny on Trial: The Evidence at Nuremberg* (Dallas: Southern Methodist Press, 1954): 28.

21. Léon Dostert, "The Instantaneous Multi-Lingual Interpreting System in the International Military Tribunal" (ts. n.d.): 3, and Alfred G. Steer, "The Simultaneous Multi-Lingual Interpreting System" (ts. n.d.): 1.

22. E. Peter Uiberall, letter to the author (Feb. 11, 1995).

23. E. Peter Uiberall, "Court Interpreting at the Nuremberg Trial" (ts. April 11, 1995): 4.

24. Hans Fritzsche, *The Sword in the Scales*. Trans. by Hildegard Springer (Stuttgart: Thiele, 1949): 80.

25. International Military Tribunal, Seventeenth Organizational Meeting (ts. Oct. 29, 1945): 16.

26. Alfred G. Steer, "The Simultaneous Multi-Lingual Interpreting System" (ts. n.d.): 1.

27. Alfred G. Steer, "Interesting Times: Memoir of Service in U.S. Navy, 1941-1947" (ts. 1992): 236.

28. Hans Fritzsche, *The Sword in the Scales*. Trans. by Hildegard Springer (Stuttgart: Thiele, 1949): 80.

29. In the video excerpts of the Nuremberg Trial (AIIC, *Nurnberg*, Geneva 1992, video-cassette) one can see the sound monitor wearing two headphones. He regulates the volume, then talks to the monitor through a special telephone.

30. E. Peter Uiberall, "Court Interpreting at the Nuremberg Trial" (ts. April 11, 1995): 4.

31. "Information Concerning Interpreters" (ts. Spring 1946): 4.

32. Didier Lazard, *Le procès de Nuremberg: récit d'un témoin* (Paris: Éditions de la Nouvelle France, 1947): 56. "Suddenly the lawyer would say, 'Your Honor, the translation is not clear. I can hear two voices at the same time. I hear French and German.' The Presiding Judge interrupted the session, and the technicians started to work on the cables." My translation.

33. Alfred G. Steer, letter to the author (Feb. 14, 1995).

34. It is interesting to read the minutes of the International Military Tribunal session of October 29, 1945, concerning the hours of sitting of the tribunal. The French proposed to work only four hours a day excluding Saturdays. The Russians proposed seven hours a day including Saturdays, a proposal which was laughed at. Judge Lawrence considered the strain that this would put on interpreters and offered a compromise. Finally the delegations agreed on six hours a day and on Saturday sessions only if necessary. The tribunal sessions were held five days a week, Monday through Friday. Saturday morning sessions were frequently arranged to "consider administrative matters or when it was decided not to break the flow of a case or a cross exam by a full week-end." (Ann and John Tusa, *The Nuremberg Trial* [London: Macmillan, 1983]: 224.) A full Saturday session was held, for example, during Wilhelm Keitel's case. Finally, the tribunal suspended its sessions for two weeks at Christmas and from August 31 to September 30, 1946. During this time the judges met to decide about the verdicts and sentences.

35. David and Margareta Bowen, "The Nuremberg Trials: Communication through Translation." *Meta* 30, 1 (1985): 75.

36. AIIC, "Vertrag und Allgemeine Vertragsbedingungen für Konferenzdolmetscher."

37. Hilary Gaskin, ed., *Eyewitnesses at Nuremberg* (London: Arms, 1990): 38.

38. E. Peter Uiberall, "Court Interpreting at the Nuremberg Trial" (ts. April 11, 1995): 3.

39. Frederick C. Treidell, Conference (AIIC, *Nurnberg*, Geneva 1992, videocassette).

40. Hilary Gaskin, ed., *Eyewitnesses at Nuremberg* (London: Arms, 1990): 45.

41. Hilary Gaskin, ed., *Eyewitnesses at Nuremberg* (London: Arms, 1990): 38.

42. Léon Dostert, "The Instantaneous Multi-Lingual Interpreting System in the International Military Tribunal" (ts. n.d.): 3.

43. Charles A. Horsky, "Memorandum for Justice Jackson" (ts. Sept. 5, 1945).

44. Mr. David Fox, of the AIIC Committee of Permanent Interpreters, Geneva, notes that the "pilot language system... was standard practice in the former Soviet Union, and is still common in Eastern Europe" (Letter to the author, Sept. 24, 1996). In conferences where AIIC conditions are respected, relay is avoided as much as possible, and the most frequently used languages (UN languages plus German and Japanese) are covered without relay.

45. E. Peter Uiberall, letter to the author (Feb. 25, 1995).

46. "Information Concerning Interpreters" (ts. Spring 1946): 3.

47. Alfred G. Steer, "The Simultaneous Multi-Lingual Interpreting System" (ts. n.d.): 4. In the video excerpts of the Nuremberg Trial the sound monitor calls the monitor with a silent telephone (AIIC, *Nurnberg*, Geneva 1992, videocassette).

48. As seen in the excerpts of the Nuremberg Trial (AIIC, *Nurnberg*, Geneva 1992, videocassette).

49. The article by Dana Schmidt reports that "within handy reach of the interpreters are little plywood disks marked 'slows' which the interpreters seize and hold up to the monitor if they cannot keep up." Interpreters did not confirm this piece of information, but signs saying "stop" and "slow" are visible in some pictures of the Nuremberg interpreters.

50. David and Margareta Bowen, "The Nuremberg Trials: Communication through Translation." *Meta* 30, 1 (1985): 75; Robert E. Conot, *Justice at Nuremberg* (New York: Harper, 1983): 84.

51. Alfred G. Steer, "The Simultaneous Multi-Lingual Interpreting System" (ts. n.d.): 3.

52. Alfred G. Steer, "The Simultaneous Multi-Lingual Interpreting System" (ts. n.d.): 4; 12 to 14 pages according to Dana A. Schmidt, "Pick Your Language." *The New York Times Magazine* 6 (Aug. 25, 1946): 24.

53. Alfred G. Steer, "The Simultaneous Multi-Lingual Interpreting System" (ts. n.d.): 4; 26 pages in Dana A. Schmidt, "Pick Your Language." *The New York Times Magazine* 6 (Aug. 25, 1946): 24.

54. As seen in the video excerpts of the Nuremberg Trial (AIIC, *Nurnberg*, Geneva 1992, videocassette).

55. International Military Tribunal, *Trial of the Major War Criminals before the International Military Tribunal, Nuremberg 14 November 1945—1 October 1946.* 4 (Nuremberg, 1947): 373-374.

56. Ann and John Tusa, *The Nuremberg Trial* (London: Macmillan, 1983): 150-151.

57. John Dos Passos, "Report from Nürnberg." *Life* (Dec. 10, 1945): 49-50.

58. Frederick C. Treidell, Conference (AIIC, *Nurnberg*, Geneva 1992, videocassette).

59. Hilary Gaskin, ed., *Eyewitnesses at Nuremberg* (London: Arms, 1990): 41.

60. Hilary Gaskin, ed., *Eyewitnesses at Nuremberg* (London: Arms, 1990): 117.

61. Alfred G. Steer, "Interesting Times: Memoir of Service in U.S. Navy, 1941-1947" (ts. 1992): 250.

62. Ann and John Tusa, *The Nuremberg Trial* (London: Macmillan, 1983): 198.

63. Alfred G. Steer, "The Simultaneous Multi-Lingual Interpreting System" (ts. n.d.): 5.

64. Hilary Gaskin, ed., *Eyewitnesses at Nuremberg* (London: Arms, 1990): 43.

65. Hilary Gaskin, ed., *Eyewitnesses at Nuremberg* (London: Arms, 1990): 39.

66. Francis Biddle, *In Brief Authority* (Garden City: Doubleday, 1962): 380.

67. Robert E. Conot, *Justice at Nuremberg* (New York: Harper, 1983): 85.

68. Francis Biddle, *In Brief Authority* (Garden City: Doubleday, 1962): 381.

69. Arkadii Iosifovich Poltorak, *Nürnberger Epilog* (Berlin: Militärverlag der DDR, 1971), qtd. in Ann and John Tusa, *The Nuremberg Trial* (London: Macmillan, 1983): 111.

70. Francis Biddle, *In Brief Authority* (Garden City: Doubleday, 1962): 374.

71. Biographical information about them in chapter 5, "Profiles of Interpreters."

72. Robert E. Conot, *Justice at Nuremberg* (New York: Harper, 1983): 85.

73. Hans Fritzsche, *The Sword in the Scales*. Trans. by Hildegard Springer (Stuttgart: Thiele, 1949): 112.

74. German for "Filthy bastard!"

75. Following this episode, one of the interpreters was called to do some extra work after session. Judge Lawrence announced that he wanted to speak to Göring in private. His defense counsel and a German-English interpreter had to be there, too. Mr. Uiberall was on duty that day and he found himself in the position of delivering a lecture on proper courtroom behavior to Hermann Göring himself (Hilary Gaskin, ed., *Eyewitnesses at Nuremberg* [London: Arms, 1990]: 85).

76. International Military Tribunal, Notes of Evidence (Dec. 12, 1945): 147.

77. Léon Dostert, "The Instantaneous Multi-Lingual Interpreting System in the International Military Tribunal" (ts. n.d.): 5.

78. Alfred G. Steer, "The Simultaneous Multi-Lingual Interpreting System" (ts. n.d.): 7.

79. Francis Biddle, *In Brief Authority* (Garden City: Doubleday, 1962): 423-424.

80. Gerhard E. Gründler and Arnim von Manikowsky, *Nuremberg ou la justice des vainqueurs*. Trans. by Herbert Lugert (Paris: Laffont, 1969): 265.

81. Hilary Gaskin, ed., *Eyewitnesses at Nuremberg* (London: Arms, 1990): 45.

82. This technique was also used during pretrial interrogations, and it had the same disadvantages. The interpreter translated consecutively for the defendants, but the only version recorded by the stenographer was in English, the language of the examiner. The original German version is lost (Telford Taylor, *Final Report to the Secretary of the Army on the Nuremberg War Crimes Trials under Control Council Law No. 10*. Washington, D.C.: Government Printing Office, 1949: 60). During the trial, Alfred Jodl's defense lawyer used this problem to his advantage. When the English minutes of Jodl's interrogation were presented in court, the lawyer objected that "the minutes were... set down in the English language. These minutes he [Jodl] never saw and he did not sign them. And now these minutes, which were compiled in English, are submitted to him in a German translation. In my opinion it is quite impossible under such circumstances to tie the defendant down to specific words which are contained in the minutes." The tribunal could not but sustain the objection (International Military Tribunal, *Trial of the Major War Criminals before the International Military Tribunal, Nuremberg 14 November 1945—1 October 1946*. 15 [Nuremberg, 1947]: 455).

83. International Military Tribunal, Executive Session (ts. Nov. 24, 1945): 2. On another occasion, as one can see from the video excerpts of the Nuremberg Trial (AIIC, *Nurnberg*, Geneva 1992, videocassette), a document is read in court. Copies (of the original?) are given to the judges, one to the defense and four to the monitor, who distributes them along the interpreters' desks.

84. International Military Tribunal, Notes of Evidence (ts. Nov. 26, 1945): 40.

85. Hans Fritzsche, *The Sword in the Scales*. Trans. by Hildegard Springer (Stuttgart: Thiele, 1949): 43.

86. This solution was first proposed by Judge Biddle in the International Military Tribunal Executive Session of November 24, 1945 at 2:30 p.m. and then adopted by the tribunal.

87. The translation difficulties and the bench ruling were seen by both prosecution and defense as a disadvantage towards them. The prosecution claimed that the ruling "greatly limited the amount of evidence that the Prosecution could introduce" (Bradley F. Smith, *Reaching Judgement at Nuremberg* [New York: Basic, 1981]: 84).

Lawrence, too, thought that this decision penalized the prosecution, because they could only put in evidence what was produced in court (International Military Tribunal, *Trial of the Major War Criminals before the International Military Tribunal, Nuremberg 14 November 1945—1 October 1946.* 5 [Nuremberg, 1947]: 24). The defense instead complained that the impact of the evidence read in court was greater. They felt greatly penalized when they presented their case and could not read out the documents. They were required to quote only the numbers of the documents they wanted to submit because at the time the defense made their case, the translation branch had caught up with the translation requests and all the translations of the documents were available. The defense complained that in this way their evidence would have less impact on the judges and the public than the prosecution's (International Military Tribunal, *Trial of the Major War Criminals before the International Military Tribunal, Nuremberg 14 November 1945—1 October 1946.* 5 [Nuremberg, 1947]: 24).

CHAPTER THREE

RELIABILITY AND IMPACT OF THE INTERPRETATION

RELIABILITY OF THE INTERPRETING SYSTEM

One of the key issues about the interpreting system was its reliability. Could the tribunal wholeheartedly trust the version of the interpreters? In order to ensure a fair trial to the defendants, it was necessary that every statement be translated correctly and accurately, and that no parts be missed or altered. The tribunal believed it could not rely totally on the translations of the interpreters, who might make mistakes. Moreover, before the beginning of the trial, it was not completely certain that the system would not break down after a few hours. For this reason, a system of recording was developed to which courtroom people could resort in cases of misunderstanding or disagreement about the translations. After the beginning of the trial, however, there were different opinions on how much this strategy worked to ensure fairness. For some, it left no room for error, while others considered it useless.

Recording, Reviewing and Printing

An important aspect for the fairness of the trial was to make sure that original testimony would be recorded and made available for consultation. Thus, in the courtroom, every word uttered was recorded regardless of the language: the recording served both to preserve historical documentary evidence and as a master check to the accuracy of translation. This was a considerable improvement in comparison to pretrial interrogations, in which only the English version given by the translator was recorded. In the courtroom the translations were recorded, too, short-hand, and the transcripts were reviewed at the end of the day. Later on, the printing of the transcript was added to the tasks of the Translation Division. The Recording, Reviewing and Printing Branches of the Translation Division were organized, financed and managed by the American delegation.

The Electrical Recording. The electrical recording was carried out by Army Signal Corps officers, who supplied the wire recorders from the U.S. Army equipment. The recorders were located in the room next to the interpreters, and were attached to the IBM microphones in the courtroom.[1] They were always set on channel one, the verbatim channel, containing the original speeches of the court, untranslated.[2] A picture of the sound recording room at the National Archives, Washington, D.C., shows two types of recording equipment: disc and tape recorders, which the caption calls disc and wire apparatus. In the picture, tape recorders and phonographic recorders (which record on discs) are visible. According to Mr. Uiberall, the verbatim channel was recorded on discs, which are now preserved at the National Archives. "All language channels (two to five) were recorded on tape with U.S. Army Signal Corps upright reel-type recorders,"[3] also visible in the picture. These tapes have deteriorated and are no longer available, so that, while the voices of the original speakers (verbatim) have survived until today, the voices of the interpreters are lost, except for some motion picture takes done in the courtroom.

In addition to the sound recording, three cameras recorded both images and sound. One was located near the witness stand, and two at the back of the room. The cameras in the back were operated outside the courtroom through glass partitions in order to eliminate interference with the proceedings. One camera was located in a side booth looking into the courtroom through a window. The other was on the other side of the sound monitor. Only one camera was allowed in the room next to the judges' bench, and was permitted to operate only at certain hours. Provisions were made for the temporary installation of floodlights for the making of motion pictures at certain predetermined moments during the progress of the trials.[4]

The Stenographic Record. Though the original voices of the interpreters are lost today, their translations have been preserved (albeit edited) because the translations coming through channels two to five were taken down shorthand by court reporters. The court reporters sat in front of the bench facing the defendants; each of them was assigned a specific language and recorded the proceedings for 15 to 20 minutes, after which he or she was relieved by a colleague. The British and

American personnel were using stenotype and stenographic machines, while the German and Russian court reporters recorded shorthand, with the Russians even using pens and inkwells. Immediately after leaving the room they would type out their recordings.

At the beginning of the trial, court members were able to get the daily transcript of a day's proceedings only after 48 hours,[5] as evident also from Lawrence's words on January 9, 1946: "The shorthand notes in German are not available the next morning but are available only some days afterwards."[6] On the same day a German lawyer complained that he had just received the transcripts of the December 18 and 19 sessions, which he considered an intolerable delay. He was told that there had been a paging error and that the transcripts had to be recopied, and that the delay was usually not that long.[7] After the first months of the trial, however, the court reporting branch was able to supply a complete stenotype record of the proceedings to all court members in each of the four languages by the end of the day. It is reported, for example, that immediately after the court session in which the prosecution made their final speeches, Göring was given the daily transcript in German by his lawyer. Already on the next day he could boast that his name had been quoted more than anyone else's in Jackson's speech.[8]

The issue of the immediate availability of transcripts was crucial. Some judges probably used the transcripts in their languages, together with their own notes, to go over the day's proceedings and debate about prosecution and defense requests. Prosecution and defense needed the transcripts to formulate their cases and to respond to each other's objections. Thus the court reporting section was required to work efficiently but, most of all, quickly.

Reviewing.   Accuracy and speed, however, did not always go along well. The stenotype record often contained mistakes. The judges complained that they were receiving transcripts full of inaccuracies. They were of course not all interpreting errors: mistakes were made by the speakers, who because of nervousness or tiredness would misread numbers, references to documents, dates, etc. Interpreting errors would also inevitably occur because of the high strain put on interpreters and, finally, stenographers too made errors of transcription.

Already before the trial, Jackson's staff contemplated the creation of a Reviewing Branch, in which the daily transcript would be checked against the sound recording in order to verify the accuracy of interpretation and of shorthand reporting. The Reviewing Branch of the Translation Division was located one floor above the courtroom. Here, the stenographic transcripts were checked against the verbatim recording. The reviewers corrected the mistakes of stenographers in the original versions, and edited and polished the translations if necessary. Discrepancies between the translation and the original were discussed with the defense if they regarded the interests of the defendants. Sometimes, when the interpreters were not satisfied with the version they had given in session, at the end of their shift they would run upstairs to the reviewing room. They asked to correct parts of their interpretation and suggested improvements.[9] The reviewing staff had to know the working languages of the tribunal and sometimes translators and interpreters themselves acted as reviewers. For a long time, the Head of the Reviewing Branch was Marguerite Wolf, who came to Nuremberg from London. She did not test out as an interpreter, and was assigned to a different Branch.

The polishing of translations and the loss of the recordings of the interpreters' voices makes it very difficult today, if not impossible, to check for the accuracy of in-court interpretation. The transcripts published in different languages that are available today possibly went through considerable editing, and they might be different from the version that the judges and the entire tribunal heard in court.

Printing.   Some time after the beginning of the trial, the judges asked Alfred Steer, then Head of the Translation Division, if it was possible to have the transcripts printed after they had been corrected and polished. Mr. Steer, together with Mr. Burton from Great Britain, set up a commission and organized the Printing Branch. However, printing presented major difficulties in war-destroyed Germany. Sigmund Roth was at the time the administrative Head of the Court Reporting and the Reviewing Branches (45 and 100 people respectively) and a close friend of Mr. Steer's. He had experience in editing and was put in charge of the printing. He found good printing facilities in the Nuremberg-Erlangen area, but paper and binding material were scarce; Roth negotiated with the Soviets to obtain them from the Russian zone of occupation. He was appointed director of the Printing Branch.[10] The printing started long after the trial had begun, almost as the trial was halfway over, and never caught up. Sigmund Roth remained in Nuremberg to finish the printing for more than a year after the sentences had been pronounced.

What was printed constitutes an extremely valuable historical record of the trial, "a six-million-word trial!":[11] 42 volumes of transcripts and associated documents plus one index volume: 5,000 copies of all volumes in English, and 2,500 copies in German, French and Russian, "a total of something in excess of 500,000 volumes. These sets were then deposited... in major libraries around the world."[12]

The key question about the Recording, Reviewing and Printing Branches is: was it necessary for the conduct of the trial to record, review and print the proceedings?

The Need for the Recording System

The whole effort of recording electrically and shorthand, then checking and double-checking the records, was aimed at providing accurate transcripts of the proceedings for the use of the participants. Leaving aside their obvious value for posterity, how important were the transcripts for the course of the trial? The answer to this question depends on the assumptions about judges' working methods. If one assumes that the transcripts were essential to the judges in formulating their judgements, then it was crucial that they receive transcripts of the exact words spoken in court, or their exact meaning in case of translations. On the other hand, if what actually mattered to the judges were only the words spoken in court, then it was more important to have the best interpretation right in the courtroom. For the latter hypothesis, the system of recording and reviewing was useless.

The defendant Hans Fritzsche thought that the whole recording and reviewing effort was pointless. He believed that the most important testimony was the one coming through the earphones, because the judges would form their opinion according to what they heard in court. For that reason, he felt it was absolutely necessary to have the best possible translation right in court, and tried as much as possible to help out the interpreters. He wrote,

> Of course every word of the proceedings was recorded somewhere or other; but what was the use of the most rigidly correct notes if our judges never saw them—if they were preserved only for posterity?[13]

Even if the simultaneous translation was later checked and corrected, Fritzsche doubted "that the Bench, for whose sole benefit every word was, in the last resort, uttered, ever had time to read these often very much altered and amended versions."[14]

Most other authors, on the other hand, believe that the system of recording and reviewing contributed to the fairness of the trial, because in the end it left no room for inaccuracies and mistakes in the transcripts. Siegfried Ramler, interpreter at Nuremberg, thinks that the correction of mistakes ensured fairness because it eliminated those errors of transcript that could have had "weighty consequences for the defendants and the outcome of the trials."[15] He is referring to the fact that the prosecution and the defense extensively used the daily transcripts to prepare their cases and their cross-examinations, and he assumes that the judges relied on the transcripts more than they did on the simultaneous translation made in court. This is why, according to him, it was crucial that the transcripts they received were the exact recording of what had been said in court.

Like Siegfried Ramler, Peter Uiberall, monitor and interpreter at Nuremberg, thinks that the judges did consult the transcripts during their deliberations. According to him, no mistranslations were left in the transcripts. These were checked and double-checked before being "printed or used by the judges as material for their considerations."[16] Finally, this opinion was shared by Colonel Gill, who told the judges before the trial that, if they had doubts about the accuracy of translation, they could resort to the electrical and manual recording, in order to have an exact knowledge of what had been said.[17]

Thus, the need for recording and reviewing depended on whether or not the judges actually consulted the transcripts in addition to what they heard in court. There was no written rule about this; in fact, "the judges received daily transcripts of the proceedings, which they studied or not according to temperament."[18]

From the sources, it appears that Hans Fritzsche was the only person to believe that the transcripts were useless and that every mistake made in court was bound to have an impact on the judges, with no chance of ever being corrected. It is possible that he was biased in his judgement because he was a defendant, or because he was never allowed in the consultation room, while interpreters were. Since it is unclear whether the judges consulted the transcripts for their deliberations, I can report about the recording and reviewing, but not on their contribution to the fairness of the trial.

The recording system had been devised to improve accuracy and to make originals available for consultation. It was thought that the interpreting system and the recording system would cope with all the problems in providing language services at the trial. And yet, there was an intrinsic aspect of interpretation that could not be solved by any practical means: its impact on the proceedings.

IMPACT OF INTERPRETATION ON THE PROCEEDINGS

One of the most important issues in the discussion of Nuremberg interpretation is its impact on the fairness of the proceedings. The whole interpreting system had been created for the right of the defendants to

follow the trial in their language; interpretation was one of the requirements for a "fair trial." Did interpretation deliver? Did it ensure a fair
trial to the defendants, as far as language is concerned? Or did it hinder
the fair course of justice, by favoring either defense or prosecution? In
the second part of this chapter, I will show how and to what extent the
interpreting system affected the trial.

The Impact of Interpretation on Examination
and Cross-Examination

Because of interpreting, lawyers and members of the court had to
speak slowly. They resented this most during examination and cross-
examination. Although some of them actually found the interpreting
system suited for examination, most lawyers complained that cross-
examination was ineffective when performed slowly and that they
were therefore penalized by interpretation. Their ignorance of foreign
languages and cultures also contributed to the weakness of their examinations, thus making the impact of interpretation on examination and
cross-examination even more dramatic.

The opinion people held of the interpreting system usually
depended on how much they knew about it. Léon Dostert, for
example, the person who introduced simultaneous interpretation to
Nuremberg, knew that the alternative to simultaneous translation was
consecutive interpretation; during examination and cross-examination the consecutive technique considerably delays the testimony and
does not allow for a quick exchange of questions and answers. Thus
he wrote that the system of simultaneous interpreting was particularly suited for cross-examination, because it maintained the "sponta-
neity and rapidity"[19] of the questioning, and because the prosecution
was able to put pressure on the witness or the defendant even though
they were speaking in different languages. David Maxwell-Fyfe, the
Chief British Prosecutor, thought that the system was working so
well that he could stop Göring from answering something he did not
ask before Göring had said a dozen words.[20] Apparently, the interpreting system made one forget that different languages were being
spoken, and counsel were even able to "call each other names"[21] in
heated debates.

Most of those who commented on the interpreting system, however, knew little about translation issues. They compared the interpreted trial to a normal trial, instead of comparing the simultaneous
system with other less efficient methods. Inevitably, they were critical

about interpretation. Lawyers often complained about the delay of translation, which was not exactly "simultaneous" with the original. The inevitable delay gave the defendants or the witnesses who understood the two languages the time to think about their answer without this appearing suspect.[22] Many of the defendants (Schacht, Fritzsche, Speer, Göring, Hess) spoke at least English besides German; they could understand the English question and then use the time of the translation to think about the answer. This is not the way a cross-examination should be carried out:

> Ideally the lawyer in a cross-exam should drive it through at the speed he dictates, not allowing the witness breathing space or a chance to draw red herrings across the line of questioning.[23]

Lawyers accustomed to the breathtaking rhythm of traditional examination felt strongly penalized. After his poor cross-examination of Hermann Göring, Justice Jackson, the U.S. Chief Prosecutor, blamed the interpreting system for his failure. Göring, he claimed, always had the possibility to say he did not understand the question because the translation was poor or not loud enough, just to gain more time to think. Göring asked to have the question rephrased in order to avoid answering it. Jackson bitterly complained that

> [Göring] could always get time to get his speech ready. You couldn't stop him. He knew English, could understand the question, and while they were interpreting it for him he already had the question from me, and was getting his answer ready.[24]

Only David Maxwell-Fyfe, the British prosecutor, seemed able to cope with this unexpected change in the rhythm of cross-examination. He thought that "this [slow pace of examination] was not a high price to pay for what was called a justice in four voices."[25] In his brilliant cross-examination of Göring, he found an ingenious way to deal with the inconvenience of the interpretation delay.

> At one point Göring was waiting for the interpretation, and [Maxwell-Fyfe] said, "Well, witness, you understand English quite well, don't you? Suppose you answer right away?"[26]

Other members of the tribunal complained about the slowness of diction imposed on them by the interpreting system and the impossibility of rapid exchange. They constantly tried to carry out their examinations at the speed they wanted, regardless of interpretation needs. On January 7, 1946, defense counsel cross-examined a German prosecution witness, von dem Bach-Zelewski. Since both counsel and witness spoke German and they could understand each other without headphones, the cross-exam was conducted very quickly. The defense lawyer was pressing the witness with quick questions in order to lead him into contradiction, and the witness answered the questions promptly. Thus interpreters had a hard time in keeping up with the pace. What the defense counsel did not understand was that his quick and skilful cross-examination was having no effect on the judges, who all relied on interpretation for understanding. The power of his cross-examination was diminished by a hurried translation. Judge Lawrence pointed out this fact to the lawyer:

> Unless counsel and the witness speak slowly and make adequate pauses between the questions and the answers, it is impossible for the interpreters to interpret properly, and the only result is that the questions and answers do not come through to the Tribunal... and everything you might think you gain by rapidity of cross-examination, you lose by the inadequacy of translation. I will repeat, that you should pause at the end of your sentences and at the end of your questions, so as to give the interpreter's voice time to come through.[27]

On behalf of the interpreters, it must be said that, if the prosecution cases turned out to be mostly weak and ineffective, it was not always because of interpretation. Another way in which the multilingual nature of the tribunal affected the proceedings was the way in which the British and American prosecution teams managed to make themselves ridiculous on certain occasions, because of their unfamiliarity with German language, history and institutions. More than once during his cross-examination of Göring, Jackson poorly pronounced German names, so that not even the interpreters could understand him. "Reichsbank" was mistaken for "Reichstag," "Woermann" for "Bormann," "Turner" for "Koerner"; Göring corrected him every time, whereupon Jackson admitted with embarrassment: "All right, my poor pronunciation."[28] Göring also repeatedly sneered at the Russian Prosecutor Rudenko's lack of German, while he had to acknowledge the excellent qualities of Maxwell-Fyfe, the British Prosecutor, who always quoted the exact German term for official posts and employed German terminology. Here is an example of Maxwell-Fyfe's elegant way to correct himself: "General Milch—I beg your pardon—Field Marshal Milch had said..."[29]

Independently of anyone's will or fault, the multilanguage nature of the trial and the need for interpretation did affect the way in which examination and cross-examination were carried out, but since this affected both prosecution and defense, it did not penalize one at the advantage of the other. The more skilled lawyers learned how to cope with interpretation, while others complained and blamed the interpreting system.

Language Issues and Their Impact on the Proceedings

Another subtle way in which interpreting affected the proceedings was linked to the very nature of the German language. Some of its features make it less suitable for simultaneous interpretation than other languages. Translating the defense's speeches from German turned out to be more difficult than other interpreting tasks. Moreover, German speakers were often slow in cooperating, and sometimes used vague and ambiguous terms on purpose, thus preventing an objective, clear translation of their speeches.

Among the features that create difficulties for interpreters is the German syntactic structure. In the German secondary clause, and with compound and modal verbs, the verb is positioned at the end of the sentence.[30] When translating into French or English, the interpreter had to change the structure of the sentence, because these languages require the verb in the first half of the sentence. How were interpreters supposed to translate the verb before they heard it? If the sentence was short, interpreters could afford to wait until they heard the verb. But with long-winded sentences, typical of legal language, the interpreter did not have the time to wait until the end of the sentence, otherwise they would lag behind and would not be able to catch up. One method to deal with this complex situation was, and still is for interpreters, to anticipate the verb, that is, to infer from the first words of the sentence and the context what the verb was going to be. Though feasible, this task required native-like knowledge of the language. Even so, most times interpreters were not able to anticipate the meaning of the sentence, because in some sentences, it becomes clear only at the end whether the sentence is negative or affirmative.[31] Interpreters developed a method to cope with this: they started the sentence with vague and general phrases and then became more specific once they heard the verb. This allowed them to keep pace with the speaker and to deliver a reasonable, even if not elegant, translation.[32]

The German counsel at Nuremberg did actually use long and complex sentences, without realizing that this would endanger the quality of the translation their speech received. Among the defendants, Hans Fritzsche was well aware of this. In his memoirs, he describes how much German speakers were ignorant of the problems of interpreters:

> Many a time I have wrung my hands in despair while a German counsel or witness, seeing the yellow flashes, would with the best of intentions pause in the middle of a sentence, a proceeding not to the slightest service to the interpreter, who was still waiting eagerly for the

verb. Often a guard would signal to me to be quiet as I tried, instinctively, to stop with a gesture some compatriot who had over-shot the one and only point at which a pause could make sense to his foreign audience. Because of this weakness, essential parts of various German arguments were entirely lost in translation and never came up for discussion at all.[33]

This statement of Fritzsche's is quite strong and, if proved right, would show that the interpretation from German could compromise the fairness to the defendants; but before we draw that conclusion, a number of factors indicate that we should be cautious. First of all, Fritzsche was probably listening to German and English, or German and Russian, in the courtroom, but it was improbable that he found inadequate the translations from German into all three other languages. Moreover, as mentioned, the judges and the prosecution received accurate translations of the daily transcripts, and assuming they read them, they would have found those "essential parts" of German arguments. Finally, Fritzsche himself is clear on this: it was not the interpreters' fault if translation from German sometimes failed. He realized that the greatest difficulty for the interpreters was the use of long sentences whose full meaning was revealed only at the end by the verb. Thus he wrote some "Suggestions for Speakers," where he proposed the use of short sentences in which the verb would appear as much as possible at the beginning. He distributed these suggestions among the defendants. Göring learned them by heart and made good use of them during direct questioning and cross-examination.

> Other prisoners started off well but forgot their good intentions from over-anxiety. Sauckel was the worst: under the strain of examination, and especially of cross-examination, more than half of what he had to say in his own defense remained untranslated. It was, quite simply, untranslatable.[34]

As this quote shows, Fritzsche was aware that interpreters could not translate a speech like Sauckel's and therefore he did not blame them. He knew that a good translation depends on the speaker as much as on the interpreter.

There was another German peculiarity the interpreters had to be careful of if they wanted to ensure fairness in their translation. It was the habit of German speakers to begin their sentences with *Ja*. While it was usually translated as "Yes," this *Ja* was often used by the speakers as a space-filler, a way to take time and think about the answer:

> Germans had a tendency to begin speaking with "*Ja*." Interpreted literally, the utterance could amount to an admission of guilt. "Did you realize that what you were doing was criminal?" a prosecutor might

> ask. *"Ja,"* the witness would reply, meaning not "Yes," but a space-filler, more accurately translated as "Well..."[35]

Peter Uiberall was particularly concerned with this problem, and once he became Chief Interpreter he instructed his staff to wait before translating *Ja* as "Yes." Interpreters had to be absolutely sure that what the witness meant was a positive reply and had to be fully aware of the consequences of their translation.

> It's completely different in word material in English from the German, and yet in a court of law this is the correct way to translate it, or else you're hanging a man, wrongly. Because once that "Yes" is in the transcript the man is stuck.[36]

Finally, the German language was also difficult to translate because of the ambiguities of the Nazi jargon. Some terms and expressions, which taken literally have an "innocent" meaning, were known to be used by the Nazis to mean criminal acts. The term *Endlösung,* for example, translated literally as "final solution," was known to be used as a euphemism for the annihilation of the Jews. This is even more evident with the term *erfassen* which means "to register" but can also be taken to mean "to seize physically."[37] In these cases, the interpreters had the responsibility to choose one of the versions and their decision would inevitably have an impact on the testimony. In his cross-examination, Göring complained more than once that his words were being translated in a way that added nuances of meaning. As a result, interpreters would find themselves at times in the position of translating an argument in court about the accuracy of their own translation.

Interpreters' Personality and Voice and Their Effect on the Proceedings

As explained above, interpretation affected the proceedings during examination and cross-examination and when translating from German. Another way in which interpretation influenced the proceedings was through interpreters' personality and voice. Through vocal inflection or other extralinguistic features they could add or eliminate nuances from the testimony. Sometimes their personality or character prevented them from translating correctly, and they had to be replaced, as described below.

From the very beginning the interpreting staff at Nuremberg realized that the personality and voice of the interpreters were not to detract from the witnesses' and defendants' testimony. The listeners had to be unaware of the interpreters and accept their voices as original.[38] This was not easy to achieve, though. Some interpreters colored the original version through vocal inflection or a particular rendering of the speech.There were instances during the trial when either the personality or the voice of the interpreter interfered with testimony. Some interpreters were unemphatic and relaxed; others spoke in a rush, dramatically. The interpreter Margot Bortlin, for example, became famous at Nuremberg for interpreting dramatically, acting every part with face and voice, smiling and frowning.[39] Differently, there was "a rather laconic interpreter who gave the shortest possible rendition of long sentences, sometimes leaving the audience wondering what they were missing."[40] Because of short renditions an interpreter was reprimanded by the Presiding Judge during the interrogation of a witness, Mr. Pine, in one of the few hilarious episodes of the trial:

> The judge got very cross about this on one occasion, and gave the interpreter a going-over in front of everybody saying, "Now look here, I want you to translate *everything* I say, *exactly*. Do you understand?" The interpreter nodded, and the judge signaled to me to proceed, saying, "Yes, Mr. Pine?," whereupon the interpreter said, "Ja, Herr Tannenbaum?"[41]

Sometimes vigorous and masculine speeches by generals such as the French Prosecutor Dubost were translated by a "stout, tenor-voiced" interpreter "with the 'refayned' and precious accents of a decaying pontiff."[42] Young women with "chirpy little voices"[43] translating rough generals also diminished the power of testimony. "On one occasion, after the aristocratic Erwin Lahousen had been interpreted by a barely educated German-American, Birkett asked, 'And what language was that?' 'Brooklynese,' Steer answered."[44]

On other occasions, the personality of interpreters, especially women, affected the proceedings because they refused to use derogatory language. This was the case when a Nazi witness described the "humane" conditions of a work camp, equipped among others with a library, a swimming pool and a brothel. The young German-English interpreter, an American woman, could not or would not translate the word "brothel," and remained silent. Lawrence intervened to ask "What was it that they had?" whereupon the masculine voice of the monitor was heard, "a BROTHEL, Your Honor!," and the courtroom burst out laughing.[45] On another occasion, a woman interpreter was on duty when "one of those concentration camp guards [was] on the stand, who was an animal. He used the most incredibly filthy, derogatory language you could imagine."[46] The interpreter refused to use such a language and rendered sentences like "You just had to piss on the Jews" (*auf die Juden pissen*) with softer expressions such as "You just had to ignore the Jews." In both cases, the interpreters had to be replaced, because their behavior was compromising the impact of such testimony on the trial. As interpreters they could not let their personality influence their translation. Alfred Steer told the latter interpreter:

> "Look," I said, "you are a servant of the court and the judges are rely-ing on your interpretation to get their opinion of what that man is say-ing. It is *your* responsibility to give an accurate, complete translation, even if it *isn't* in harmony with your ideas."[47]

It might seem from the discussion above that, at some points, interpretation and its problems were a disadvantage to the defendants. However, the language situation could just as well be exploited by the defendants to their advantage. Some, as mentioned before, did not: they were so nervous on the witness stand that part of what they said remained untranslated. But others were more skilled. First among them, Hermann Göring.

The Defendants and Interpretation

The situation created by interpretation at the Nuremberg Trial was new and unfamiliar to the court members. It created possibilities that no one thought could be exploited for one's own advantage, until Hermann Göring took the stand. He skilfully exploited the language situation and the uneasiness of the tribunal about running a four-language trial. He fully realized the potential of the interpreting system and alternately praised it and criticized it for the impact it had on him. Ironically, in the end, the interpreting system seemed to take its revenge on Göring.

During his cross-examination, Göring adopted strategies to gain time and think about his answers, and to make prosecutors lose their temper. This technique worked extremely well, especially with the American Prosecutor Robert Jackson, who suffered a humiliating defeat on the first day of his cross-examination. Göring listened patiently to Jackson's long and complicated questions, including lengthy quotations from documents; then, at least a dozen times, he politely asked Jackson to repeat or reword his questions, claiming that the simultaneous trans-lation was either incomprehensible or inadequate. He often asked to have his question retranslated. As a sign of contempt, he sometimes said that the German translation of the question was not clear, but that he was able to answer all the same.[48]

Göring was also quick in exploiting one of the major weak-nesses of the interpreting system, which has been described earlier: the double translation, that is, when a German original document had been translated into English for the use of the prosecution and was then retranslated into German for the defendants in the courtroom. Of course, after the second translation, the text was slightly different from the original. When Göring pointed out to the court that he could not be asked to recognize his words after a double translation, he was given the German original text. This was far from being a solution, because the English-into-German interpreter had not been given the same original text. Thus Göring complained that the interpretation was biased to his disadvantage:

> That quotation has not been translated by the interpreter as it is written down here in the original. The interpreter who is translating your words into German is using many strong expressions which are not contained in this document.[49]

Göring also played on the fact that he knew both English and German, while Jackson was not familiar with German at all. More than once Göring pointed out inaccuracies in the English translation of German documents. For example, during the episode that became famous as the "translation mistake," Jackson had to withdraw an important document from the evidence, which, according to him, should have proved the German intention to free the Rhineland early in 1935. The original document read *"Freimachung des Rheins,"* which means "clearing of the Rhine" but had been translated as "liberation of the Rhine" in the English translation of the document. This notwithstanding, the document was not mistranslated, but Jackson, or someone on his staff, mistook the term "Rhine" for "Rhineland," a blatant mistake that did not escape the clever eye of Göring.[50] When Jackson triumphantly presented the document as a proof of the German intention to free the Rhineland, Göring mercilessly lectured Jackson on why he was wrong and showed off his translation skills.

Göring also showed Jackson that, when reading from another document, he or the interpreter was mistaking *Endlösung* "final solution" for *Gesamtlösung* "total solution."[51] Göring had been given the original German document and offered to give the "correct" translation:

> Da Göring in der Dolmetscherübersetzung wohl Unstimmigkeiten mit dem ihm vorliegenden deutschen Original entdeckt hatte, hatte er die Verlesung des Dokumentes mit Einwilligung Jacksons selbst übernommen und hierbei sehr geschickt gleich Erläuterungen eingeflochten... Damit wurde für den Zuhörer, insbesondere den Ausländer, der Unterschied zwischen Gesamtlösung (1. Absatz), die sich auf Auswanderung und Evakuirung bezieht, und der angestrebten Endlösung verwischt.[52]

He adopted the same strategy for the German word *nieder-schlagen*. Jackson was accusing Göring of having "suppressed" or "quashed" some penal proceedings, while Göring claimed that the correct translation of *niederschlagen* is "to suspend" a penal proceeding, which is a legal action.[53] He repeated his claim that the translations added meaning to his words and were biased to his disadvantage.

As part of his dialectic strategy, Göring was taking advantage of the linguistic weakness of the tribunal and his most vulnerable victim, ironically, had been one of the strongest supporters of the interpreting system, Justice Jackson. Göring revealed his game in his prison cell, after the cross-examination:

> Er war stolz auf seine dialektische Leistung in der Verhandlung. "Da habe ich den Jackson glänzend ausmanövriert!" sagte er schmunzelnd. "Besser könnte kein Anwalt das Dokument behandeln."[54]

The bench played along with his game because they did not feel secure about the language services and facilities. They should have made full use of their language staff instead of letting Göring play the expert on translation matters.[55] It was not so much a matter of translation to Göring, but a final revenge he wanted to take on the Allies before his death sentence. He wanted to ridicule them in front of the world, and express his scorn at the show trial they had staged. To do this, he was ready to exploit any weakness of the tribunal to his advantage.

Many quotations of Göring's show that, from the start, he was aware of the impact of interpretation on the trial. The epigraphy of this book, "Of course I want counsel. But it is even more important to have a good interpreter,"[56] shows the importance he attributed to good communication. In two other quotes (possibly reporting the same sentence by him) Göring considers the dramatic impact of interpretation on his own life:

> Dr. Stefan F. Horn, one of the translators, quotes [Göring] as saying to the simultaneous interpreters "You are shortening my life by several years."[57]

> After the trial started, Hermann Göring was overheard to say: "This system is very efficient, but it will also shorten my life!"[58]

There are two possible explanations of what Göring meant when he said that interpreting shortened his life. Maybe he appreciated the efficiency of the interpreting system, thanks to which the trial lasted one year instead of four; thus his death sentence (of which he was sure from the beginning) was to be pronounced three years earlier because of simultaneous interpreting. Or maybe he meant that interpreters and translators were rendering his testimony into other languages in such a way as to make his death sentence more likely. For example, when given the choice to translate *erfassen* with either "register" or "seize," they would prefer the more incriminating version for him.

Göring and other defendants also made use of the interpreting system to show what they thought about the trial. Göring and Hess took off their headphones as the Russian Prosecutor Rudenko delivered his opening speech. They meant with that gesture that it was not worth listening to. Göring also showed his anger and fury during the cross-examination of the German witness Dahlerus by pulling at the cord of the headphones. A guard had to take it from his hands before he ripped it off.[59] Many defendants also removed their headphones when evidence of the living conditions in concentration camps was given, as if they could not bear or care to hear about the atrocities.

As mentioned earlier, Göring intended to take revenge on the Allies by exploiting the weakness of the interpreting system. Paradoxically, it was the interpreting system that took its "revenge"[60] on Göring on the day the sentences were read. He was the first to come in, alone, to hear his sentence. The eyes of the visitors were on him. When Lawrence started to speak, Göring made a sign. He could not hear the translation.

> Le silence l'entoure, l'oppresse, le saisit, le paralyse, l'empêche de se mouvoir et de penser. C'est un océan de silence où il s'enfonce impuissant, ridicule, désespéré, comme un sourd qui saurait qu'on dit du mal de lui... la technique a bien choisi le moment de sa vengeance. Lord Justice pourrait crier dans son micro: Goering ne s'entendrait pas condamner à mort.[61]

> At another time, the incident would have seemed ridiculous, a mere triviality. At such moment it seemed dreadful, heart stopping... At last Göring signaled that all was well. Lawrence began to read again. Göring stood rigid as the last words of the translator reached him: "Tode durch den Strang."[62]

In conclusion, interpretation did have an impact on the proceedings. It changed the way examination and cross-examination were carried out, it filtered information between defense, defendants, prosecution and bench, it added a third party to the communication between speakers and listeners. But overall its limits applied to all those who relied on translation, such as prosecution, defense, defendants as well as judges; finally, transcripts were available to all participants.

Not everyone could see both virtues and shortcomings of the interpreting system. Many saw either one or the other. Göring's dual attitude to the interpreting system is mirrored by the comments of court members, split between praise and complaint.

Comments on Interpretation

The interpreting system had a major impact on the media and the public. The media and the language personnel expressed the most enthusiastic comments about it, for different reasons. The media were impressed by its results and did not know about its shortcomings. Interpreters knew they were getting good results *despite* its shortcomings. On the other hand, most criticism came from those who focused on minor aspects more than on the overall picture. They were court members commenting on minor inconveniences created by interpretation. Only a few commented on the actual shortcomings of the system. On the whole, the most widespread judgement on the interpretation was that it worked admirably:

> A four-power trial which could have been a farce in four languages had turned out to be (in the first eleven days) a triumph of orderly jurisprudence.[63]

Of course simultaneous interpreting had its imperfections and created inconvenience, but it saved a great amount of time. The charter of the tribunal called for a prompt trial and the simultaneous translation system made the trial work swiftly and smoothly, and considerably lightened the task of the tribunal. Many journalists and authors present at the sessions commented on the high quality and extraordinary proficiency of the interpreters. They considered it "a miracle like Pentecost."[64] People more knowledgeable about translation issues, such as language personnel, were astonished at its success, considering "the limitless scope of the issues involved, technicalities of politics, military terms or the empty phrases of Nazi jargon."[65] It was noticed that with excellent interpreters, even the liveliness of the original speech could be reproduced through the modulation of the voice. The interpreters into German were especially praised, as were those into Russian. In one of the Subsequent Proceedings, Ohlendorff, one of the defendants condemned to death, asked for permission to write a letter of appreciation to the interpreters, who, he felt, had given him the chance to understand and be understood in court. He thought he had thus been given a fair trial.[66] Jackson, too, was one of those who focused on the overall picture rather than on details; despite his complaints about its impact on cross-examination, he was able to see that interpretation as a whole had made the trial possible:

> The success and smooth working of this trial is due in no small measure to the system of interpretation and the high quality of the interpreters who have been assembled to operate it.[67]

Critical remarks concerning the interpretation system were addressed either to the interpretation itself or to the interpreters. The defendant Hans Fritzsche, who greatly admired the work of the interpreters, commented on the very nature of simultaneous interpreting and highlighted its shortcomings. He knew that translation is a difficult task because of the different natures of languages, and thought that it becomes almost impossible when done extempore by an interpreter. The interpreter is not allowed time to stop and think, and does not have enough time to catch the deep meaning of what is being said. According to Fritzsche this was an insidious defect that manifested itself from the very beginning, and became more and more evident as the trial proceeded.[68]

More criticism accompanied this critical judgement by Fritzsche. One of the German lawyers once complained that while it is good that interpreters only have one sentence of *décalage*, this implies a loss of accuracy in form and substance. Basically, the interpreters do not have time to pay attention to and reproduce the nuances of the speech, so that the drama of the trial is lost.[69] This inevitable defect of simultaneous translation was noticed by other authors, too, who complained that interpreting can never be completely accurate and that sometimes part of the meaning is lost. Finally, it was recognized by the interpreters themselves, who knew that simultaneous interpreting can never be perfect, meaning by perfection the exact rendition of every single detail of the original text.

On other occasions, the criticism was directed to the interpreters themselves, rather than to the system. Objections were raised as to the accuracy of translation, either by the defendants, by counsel or by the prosecution. Some journalists wrote harsh judgements about the interpreters' performance, referring to the translation as "gibberish"[70] or "inadequate."[71] Interpreters were also criticized for filling in the interpretation either by their choice of words or by vocal inflection, or were criticized because of their voice—for example, a female voice translating a general. Some of them were criticized because of their linguistic abilities, such as the Soviet interpreters, whose performance, according to the Nuremberg interpreter George Vassiltchikov, was considered poor.[72] The American interpreters into German were said to lack fluency and vocabulary and their translations were a disadvantage for the Germans who depended on them for understanding.[73]

The harshest critic of interpreters was undoubtedly Birkett, the British Alternate Member of the bench. His English, according to those who knew him, was of a rare purity and exactitude. He condemned the use of American English terms such as "argumentation," "orientation," "motivation" and "finalize" as "crimes against humanity," just like those with which the defendants were charged. He left sour remarks on the interpreters in his memoirs. The following quotes show Birkett's low tolerance for what he perceived as low quality of language, and they reveal his profound frustration with interpreters' renditions and with the trial itself.

> When a perfectly futile cross-examination is combined with a translation which murders the English language, then the misery of the Bench is almost insupportable.[74]

> 23 April. The translators generally may know the outlines of both languages, German and English, but in general they have no sense at all of the meaning of words.[75]

> The questions themselves are extremely difficult to follow, but they are most fearfully mangled in translation by the worst interpreter the world has ever known... Irritation, I suppose, is the chief feeling, for not only is the whole proceeding a grave and wicked waste of time, but the illiterate translation is really a torture of the spirit.[76]

> But translators are a race apart—touchy, vain, unaccountable, full of vagaries, puffed up with self-importance of the most explosive kind, inexpressibly egotistical, and, as a rule, violent opponents of soap and sunlight...[77]

Finally, some criticism addressed to the interpretation was so extreme as to be almost ridiculous. After the sentences, Fritz Saukel's defense counsel objected that his client "had been sentenced purely as a result of a mistranslation of one document,"[78] while it is obvious that no defendant was sentenced merely on the basis of one document. Another text claims that there were innumerable mistranslations leading to the incrimination of the defendants. A closer look at the text reveals the revisionist attitude of the author, who is more interested in rehabilitating the image of the Nazi criminals than in translation issues.[79]

In conclusion, remarks such as Fritzsche's on the real shortcomings of simultaneous interpreting were surely valid, but were not helpful because there was no viable alternative to simultaneous interpreting for Nuremberg. Criticism by people who were not knowledgeable about the system was equally useless. Ironically, the soundest remarks about the interpreting weaknesses, such as double translation, turned out to be those made by Göring, who was more interested in exploiting them than correcting them.

Notes

1. Horsky to Justice Jackson, Telegram 7099 (ts. Aug. 22, 1945).
2. The discs with the complete original recording of the trial proceedings are at the National Archives in Washington, D.C.
3. E. Peter Uiberall, letter to the author (May 21, 1996).
4. Blake to Justice Jackson, Telegram 7100 (ts. Aug. 22, 1945). The official film recording of the trial is now at the Imperial War Museum in London.
5. Ann and John Tusa, *The Nuremberg Trial* (London: Macmillan, 1983): 248.
6. International Military Tribunal, *Trial of the Major War Criminals before the International Military Tribunal, Nuremberg, 14 November 1945—1 October 1946.* 5 (Nuremberg, 1947): 24.
7. International Military Tribunal, *Trial of the Major War Criminals before the International Military Tribunal, Nuremberg, 14 November 1945—1 October 1946.* 5 (Nuremberg, 1947): 25.
8. Ann and John Tusa, *The Nuremberg Trial* (London: Macmillan, 1983): 421.
9. Hilary Gaskin, ed., *Eyewitnesses at Nuremberg* (London: Arms, 1990): 47.
10. Alfred G. Steer, "Interesting Times: Memoir of Service in U.S. Navy, 1941-1947" (ts. 1992): 266-269.
11. Robert W. Cooper, *The Nuremberg Trial* (Harmondsworth: Penguin, 1947): 148.
12. Alfred G. Steer, "Interesting Times: Memoir of Service in U.S. Navy, 1941-1947" (ts. 1992): 266.
13. Hans Fritzsche, *The Sword in the Scales: As Told to Hildegard Springer.* Trans. by D. Pyke and H. Fraenkel (London: Wingate, 1953): 83.
14. Hans Fritzsche, *The Sword in the Scales: As Told to Hildegard Springer.* Trans. by D. Pyke and H. Fraenkel (London: Wingate, 1953): 83.
15. Siegfried Ramler, "Origins and Challenges of Simultaneous Interpretation: The Nuremberg Trial Experience." *Languages at Crossroads*, American Translators Association. Ed. by Deanna L. Hammond (Medford: Learned Information, 1988): 439.
16. Hilary Gaskin, ed., *Eyewitnesses at Nuremberg* (London: Arms, 1990): 47.
17. International Military Tribunal, Seventeenth Organizational Meeting (ts. Oct. 29, 1945): 10.
18. Ann and John Tusa, *The Nuremberg Trial* (London: Macmillan, 1983): 446.
19. Léon Dostert, "The Instantaneous Multi-Lingual Interpreting System in the International Military Tribunal" (ts. n.d.): 4.
20. David Maxwell-Fyfe Kilmuir, *Political Adventure: The Memoirs of the Earl of Kilmuir* (London: Weidenfeld, 1964): 97.
21. "Information Concerning Interpreters" (ts. Spring 1946): 3.
22. Gerhard E. Gründler and Arnim von Manikowsky, *Nuremberg ou la justice des vainqueurs.* Trans. by Herbert Lugert (Paris: Laffont, 1969): 134.
23. Ann and John Tusa, *The Nuremberg Trial* (London: Macmillan, 1983): 266.
24. Eugene C. Gerhardt, *America's Advocate: Robert H. Jackson* (Indianapolis: Bobbs, 1958): 397.
25. David Maxwell-Fyfe Kilmuir, *Political Adventure: The Memoirs of the Earl of Kilmuir* (London: Weidenfeld, 1964): 97.

26. Hilary Gaskin, ed., *Eyewitnesses at Nuremberg* (London: Arms, 1990): 87.

27. International Military Tribunal, *Trial of the Major War Criminals before the International Military Tribunal, Nuremberg, 14 November 1945—1 October 1946.* 4 (Nuremberg, 1947): 489-490.

28. International Military Tribunal, *Trial of the Major War Criminals before the International Military Tribunal, Nuremberg, 14 November 1945—1 October 1946.* 9 (Nuremberg, 1947): 448, 504, 546, 505.

29. International Military Tribunal, *Trial of the Major War Criminals before the International Military Tribunal, Nuremberg, 14 November 1945—1 October 1946.* 10 (Nuremberg, 1947): 547.

30. For example, the sentence "I think he went to England after the war" reads in German "Ich glaube, daß er nach dem Krieg nach England *gefahren ist*"; the sentence "I never talked to him during the trial" is translated as "Ich habe mit ihm während des Prozesses niemals *gesprochen.*" Sometimes the verb is positioned at the end for emphasis. For example: "The sentence in English might be 'I deny the knowledge of the existence of the death camps.' But what the interpreter heard was 'Of the existence of the death camps all knowledge I deny.'" (Joseph E. Persico, *Nuremberg: Infamy on Trial* [New York: Viking-Penguin, 1994]: 112.)

31. The sentence "I haven't talked to him since the beginning of the war" is in German "Ich habe mit ihm seit Anfang des Krieges *nicht* gesprochen."

32. Siegfried Ramler, "Origins and Challenges of Simultaneous Interpretation: The Nuremberg Trial Experience." *Languages at Crossroads,* American Translators Association. Ed. by Deanna L. Hammond (Medford: Learned Information, 1988): 438.

33. Hans Fritzsche, *The Sword in the Scales: As Told to Hildegard Springer.* Trans. by D. Pyke and H. Fraenkel (London: Wingate, 1953): 82.

34. Hans Fritzsche, *The Sword in the Scales: As Told to Hildegard Springer.* Trans. D. Pyke and H. Fraenkel (London: Wingate, 1953): 83.

35. Joseph E. Persico, *Nuremberg: Infamy on Trial* (New York: Viking-Penguin, 1994): 263.

36. Hilary Gaskin, ed., *Eyewitnesses at Nuremberg* (London: Arms, 1990): 47.

37. Siegfried Ramler, "Origins and Challenges of Simultaneous Interpretation: The Nuremberg Trial Experience." *Languages at Crossroads,* American Translators Association. Ed. by Deanna L. Hammond (Medford: Learned Information, 1988): 439.

38. Siegfried Ramler, "Origins and Challenges of Simultaneous Interpretation: The Nuremberg Trial Experience." *Languages at Crossroads,* American Translators Association. Ed. by Deanna L. Hammond (Medford: Learned Information, 1988): 439.

39. Francis Biddle, *In Brief Authority* (Garden City: Doubleday, 1962): 398.

40. Siegfried Ramler, "Origins and Challenges of Simultaneous Interpretation: The Nuremberg Trial Experience." *Languages at Crossroads*, American Translators Association. Ed. by Deanna L. Hammond (Medford: Learned Information, 1988): 439.

41. Mr. Pine in Hilary Gaskin, ed., *Eyewitnesses at Nuremberg* (London: Arms, 1990): 92-93.

42. Montgomery H. Hyde, Lord Justice: *The Life and Times of Lord Birkett of Ulverston* (New York: Random, 1964): 521.

43. Joseph E. Persico, *Nuremberg: Infamy on Trial* (New York: Viking-Penguin, 1994): 263.

44. Joseph E. Persico, *Nuremberg: Infamy on Trial* (New York: Viking-Penguin, 1994): 263. Birkett, a purist of the English language, was the British Alternate Member of the bench and Alfred Steer the monitor on duty. Erwin Lahousen was a German aristocrat called to testify as witness at the trial.

45. Elisabeth Heyward, interview (AIIC, *Nurnberg*, Geneva, 1992, videocassette). A different version of the same incident is to be found in Tusa, who quote from Biddle's memoirs, *In Brief Authority*. The SS Judge Morgen on the stand, describing conditions at the concentration camp Buchenwald, listed its facilities: a wonderful view, lawns and flower beds, a huge library, regular mail service, cinema, admirable sports facilities and a brothel. "Everyone in the courtroom burst out laughing. Lawrence, whom Biddle suspected had been dozing, inquired what the witness had said. Biddle, whose stomach had turned on the microphone in front of him, was heard to say, 'Brothel, Geoffrey, brothel.' 'What?' 'Bordello, brothel, whorehouse.' The laughter increased." (Ann and John Tusa, *The Nuremberg Trial* [London: Macmillan, 1983]: 434).

46. Hilary Gaskin, ed., *Eyewitnesses at Nuremberg* (London: Arms, 1990): 41.

47. Hilary Gaskin, ed., *Eyewitnesses at Nuremberg* (London: Arms, 1990): 41.

48. International Military Tribunal, *Trial of the Major War Criminals before the International Military Tribunal, Nuremberg, 14 November 1945—1 October 1946*. 9 (Nuremberg, 1947): 419-420.

49. International Military Tribunal, *Trial of the Major War Criminals before the International Military Tribunal, Nuremberg, 14 November 1945—1 October 1946*. 9 (Nuremberg, 1947): 419, 420.

50. International Military Tribunal, *Trial of the Major War Criminals before the International Military Tribunal, Nuremberg, 14 November 1945—1 October 1946*. 9 (Nuremberg, 1947): 506-507. It must be said that the document was suspect: within a list of seemingly innocent instructions, the expression *Freimachung des Rheins* was the only item in inverted commas.

51. International Military Tribunal, *Trial of the Major War Criminals before the International Military Tribunal, Nuremberg, 14 November 1945—1 October 1946*. 9 (Nuremberg, 1947): 519-520.

52. Werner Bross, *Gespräche mit Hermann Göring während der Nürnberger Prozesse* (Flensburg: Wolff, 1950): 235-236. "Göring discovered many discrepancies between the original German text he had been given and the simultaneous translation. He skilfully offered to translate the German text himself into English, and was able to introduce explanations in the translation [that changed the incriminating nature of the text]. In this way, he succeeded in blurring the difference between 'total solution' (first paragraph), which refers to evacuation and displacement, and the desired 'final solution.'" My translation.

53. International Military Tribunal, *Trial of the Major War Criminals before the International Military Tribunal, Nuremberg, 14 November 1945—1 October 1946*. 9 (Nuremberg, 1947): 524.

54. Werner Bross, *Gespräche mit Hermann Göring während der Nürnberger Prozesse* (Flensburg: Wolff, 1950): 236. "He was proud of his dialectic performance in the cross-examination. 'I really outmaneuvered that Jackson!' he said triumphant. 'No lawyer could have handled that document better than I did.'" My translation.

55. David and Margareta Bowen, "The Nuremberg Trials: Communication through Translation." *Meta* 30, 1 (1985): 77.

56. "Germany: The Defendants." *Time* (Oct. 29, 1945): 38.

57. David and Margareta Bowen, "The Nuremberg Trials: Communication through Translation." *Meta* 30, 1 (1985): 77.

58. Siegfried Ramler, "Origins and Challenges of Simultaneous Interpretation: The Nuremberg Trial Experience." *Languages at Crossroads,* American Translators Association. Ed. by Deanna L. Hammond (Medford: Learned Information, 1988): 438.

59. Ann and John Tusa, *The Nuremberg Trial* (London: Macmillan, 1983): 266. Dahlerus had been called by the defense but his cross-examination was such a failure that it turned out to be incriminating for the defendants.

60. Didier Lazard, *Le procès de Nuremberg: récit d'un témoin* (Paris: Éditions de la Nouvelle France, 1947): 57.

61. Didier Lazard, *Le procès de Nuremberg: récit d'un témoin* (Paris: Éditions de la Nouvelle France, 1947): 56-57. "Silence surrounds and oppresses him, paralyzing his movements and thoughts. He is drowning into an ocean of silence, impotent, ridiculed, desperate, like a deaf man who knows they are making fun of him... the equipment had chosen the right moment to take its revenge. Lord Justice could shout into the microphone: Göring wouldn't hear his own death sentence." My translation.

62. Ann and John Tusa, *The Nuremberg Trial* (London: Macmillan, 1983): 471. "Death by hanging."

63. "The Chalice of Nürnberg." *Time* (Nov. 23, 1945): 4.

64. Ann and John Tusa, *The Nuremberg Trial* (London: Macmillan, 1983): 219.

65. Robert W. Cooper, *The Nuremberg Trial* (Harmondsworth: Penguin, 1947): 149.

66. Hilary Gaskin, ed., *Eyewitnesses at Nuremberg* (London: Arms, 1990): 117.

67. C.L. Sulzberger, "Jackson Stresses Allies' Unity." *The New York Times* (March 10, 1946): 5.

68. Hans Fritzsche, *The Sword in the Scales: As Told to Hildegard Springer.* Trans. by D. Pyke and H. Fraenkel (London: Wingate, 1953): 81.

69. Gerhard E. Gründler and Arnim von Manikowsky, *Nuremberg ou la justice des vainqueurs.* Trans. by Herbert Lugert (Paris: Laffont, 1969): 134.

70. "British Case at Nuremberg." *The Times* (Dec. 3, 1945): 4.

71. "British Case at Nuremberg." *The Times* (Dec. 3, 1945): 4.

72. Ann and John Tusa, *The Nuremberg Trial* (London: Macmillan, 1983): 219.

73. Ann and John Tusa, *The Nuremberg Trial* (London: Macmillan, 1983): 219. On the other hand, Cooper (Robert W. Cooper, *The Nuremberg Trial* [Harmondsworth: Penguin, 1947]: 150) says that the interpretation into German was especially well done, and Mr. Uiberall says the Russians were all excellent interpreters (Hilary Gaskin, ed., *Eyewitnesses at Nuremberg* [London: Arms, 1990]: 70).

74. Montgomery H. Hyde, *Lord Justice: The Life and Times of Lord Birkett of Ulverston* (New York: Random, 1964): 517.

75. Montgomery H. Hyde, *Lord Justice: The Life and Times of Lord Birkett of Ulverston* (New York: Random, 1964): 515.

76. Montgomery H. Hyde, *Lord Justice: The Life and Times of Lord Birkett of Ulver-ston* (New York: Random, 1964): 520.

77. Montgomery H. Hyde, *Lord Justice: The Life and Times of Lord Birkett of Ulver-ston* (New York: Random, 1964): 521.

78. Ann and John Tusa, *The Nuremberg Trial* (London: Macmillan, 1983): 479.

79. Richard E. Harwood, *Nuremberg and Other War Crimes Trials: A New Look* (Southam: Historical Review Press, 1978).

CHAPTER FOUR

LIFE OUTSIDE THE COURTROOM

Obviously, there was much more to interpreters' experience in Nuremberg than their place and performance in the courtroom. In an effort to
give a well-rounded picture of the experience of the interpreters in
Nuremberg, this chapter explores the more human part of their Nuremberg stay and their lives off-court: how they spent their time and pay-
check, where they lived and what relationships existed among themselves
and with other court members.

Interpreters' Pay

The U.S. was by far the richest country among the Allied nations. Their
salaries were high, though the distribution was unfair. The French,
Russian and British economies had been destroyed by the war, so that it is
not surprising that they were not paying as generous salaries as the U.S.,
and did not have as much personnel. As a result, the Americans ended up
paying most of the costs of the language services, and this fact had a
remarkable impact on the organization of the Subsequent Proceedings.

Before the beginning of the trial the delegations agreed that the
U.S., being the host nation at Nuremberg, would provide and finance the
Translation Division.[1] Each country would provide the personnel for language services into its own language, with the British and the Americans
sharing the responsibility for German. Interpreters would be paid by the
delegation that hired them, which corresponded to their desk (for example, France paid for the French desk, the U.S.S.R. for the Russian desk).

As for U.S. personnel pay, from the beginning the U.S. Office of
Chief of Counsel realized that the high-caliber personnel they needed
would be entitled to substantial compensation. They knew that the

functioning of the system and the success of the trial itself depended upon the interpreters and did not want to economize on their fees. But the compensation presented problems. Charles Horsky, Jackson's executive, suggested putting translators and interpreters on the payroll of the Overseas Branch of the War Department; if that was not feasible he suggested creating an *ad hoc* sum from the President's fund.[2]

Neither of the two suggestions worked, however, and anarchy ruled at the U.S. payroll office. There were no standards for pay. Most of the time, the procedure for U.S. personnel was to continue the person's former pay, which was an unfair system. The order read:

> Employees of the State Department or other governmental agencies who are recruited may come on temporary duty and in this case would continue to be paid by their present employer.[3]

With this method, an interpreter hired as Army PFC (private first class, the lowest U.S. Army grade) would receive about $85 a month, and would sit next to, and do the same job as, the top legal expert from the Department of Justice, hired at the top civil service salary of $10,000 per year.[4] Later on, when the division realized that interpreters needed to be paid enough so that their services could be retained, the salaries were increased. This was the suggestion Alfred Steer, then Head of the Translation Division, put forward in 1946 in the document "Simultaneous Multi-Lingual Interpreting System," where he suggested paying interpreters between CAF 9 and CAF 11. CAF (clerk administrative fiscal) was the now outmoded way to classify civil service employees. After his suggestion, the interpreters usually received a CAF-11 pay, which at the time was relatively high. CAF 1, the lowest grade, corresponded to $500-$640 a year, CAF 2 about $200 more, and the highest level was CAF 15, which was paid around $12,000 a year. For comparison, "in the late 1940's and early 1950's fees for interpreting were generally $25 per day in 'large teams,' and $36-40 in small teams."[5]

The personnel index cards of some Nuremberg interpreters show that most of them in 1945 were paid between $3,000 and $4,500, with the exception of George (Youri) Khlebnikov ($1,200) and Haakon Chevalier ($6,230). Siegfried Ramler remembers being given the CAF-11 rate, and being paid a yearly salary of about $3,000.[6] Frederick Treidell remembers that some interpreters, including himself, who were hired as CWS 9 (Continental Wage Schedule), advanced to CWS 11 after a few months, which mainly meant better accommodations, especially at the Grand Hotel.[7]

U.S. interpreters and court personnel were paid in special occupation dollars, which were only valid to purchase American goods, for example, at the PX in the courthouse.[8] At this store, interpreters and other court personnel could find American products that were not to be found otherwise on the German market. Even so, there was scarcity of some products, such as toothpaste. On Fridays, regardless of the origin of their pay, interpreters received PX supplies from the Americans, goods that were otherwise impossible to find, such as chocolate, women's stockings,[9] soap, cigarettes and possibly razor blades.[10]

From the beginning, the U.S. Office of Chief of Counsel doubted that other delegations would be able to provide their personnel. At first, this did not seem to affect them. They thought that if a country did not provide personnel for their own language, they would be the only sufferer.[11] It turned out that the functioning of the whole system was slowed down and even endangered if just one court reporter or interpreter was missing or failing. Americans therefore made up for the deficiencies of other countries. They often hired additional personnel for other languages and ended up paying most of the costs of the language services. Both British and French were close with money, according to the Americans. For this reason, the British had fewer personnel than the U.S. delegation; for example, 40 percent of the interpreters at the English desk were British, and the rest Americans.[12]

They noticed that, for example, French personnel were greatly underpaid, and for this reason it was difficult to retain their services. In agreement with the French, the Americans at first "lent" personnel to the French delegation, that is, into-French personnel were hired by the Americans and paid by the French. Later on, this solution was dropped and most into-French personnel were paid directly by the Americans. George (Youri) Khlebnikov and Marie-France Skuncke, for example, worked for the French team but were paid by the U.S. They were rather lucky that it was so, because how well interpreters lived depended on who was paying them.[13] The French Foreign Ministry paid much lower salaries. In the Personnel List of the Translation Division, which includes translators, stenographers and reviewers as well as interpreters, salaries in French *francs* range from a minimum of Fr 8,000 to a maximum of Fr 30,000, with most personnel being paid either Fr 20,000 or Fr 26,000.[14]

No details were found about the salaries paid by the British and the Russians. The document listing personnel pay at Nuremberg, "Current Translating Division Personnel List," does not include the Russian teams (they were not part of the Translation Division) and does not mention the pay of British personnel.

The issue of who was paying personnel salaries and the costs of language services is quite important for its repercussions on the organization of the Subsequent Proceedings. In 1946, Alfred Steer, Head of the Translation Division, was asked to draft a document showing the sharing of the financial burden of the Translation Division among the four powers ("Participation of Allied Delegations in the Work of the Translating Division"). He reported that the French and the Russians had supplied about 80 percent of the personnel they were supposed to hire, and the British only 20 percent. The deficiencies had been made up by the Americans, who ended up paying 70 percent of the salaries of the whole division.

After the trial, the American administration considered whether or not to carry out the trials of the lesser Nazis on an international basis. Mr. Steer's report was on Truman's desk when he decided not to conduct other four-power four-language trials: considering the financial burden carried by the United States only for the language services, the U.S. would have ended up paying most of the costs of the Subsequent Proceedings.[15] It was decided that each Allied country would try the captured Nazis individually, in their zone of occupation. In fact, the U.S. was the only country to conduct Subsequent Proceedings, which were composed solely of U.S. judges and held only in English and German.

Housing and Board

Housing and board were also organized by the Americans and posed a number of problems. First of all, Americans had to face the problem of where to house and feed the enormous population of newly arrived soldiers, court members and their families, press correspondents, etc. Nuremberg was a war-destroyed city; only a few buildings had been spared from the bombs. Transportation was difficult. Americans took over the Grand Hotel, located near the railroad station, which was once the most luxurious hotel in Nuremberg but had been bomb-damaged during the war. One of the wings had been hit and the gap in the wall had been covered with canvas. This hotel and the Reichspost Hotel were used as billets for personnel of the U.S. Office of Chief of Counsel. In addition, the Army commandeered many of the German houses that were still standing. As for board, no food was to be found on the German market, and Americans had to import it from the U.S.

At the meeting of the International Military Tribunal of October 29, 1945, Gill, of the U.S. Office of Chief of Counsel, explained that the Americans were taking the responsibility for housing interpreters of every nation. At first they billeted them in the Grand Hotel, which after repairs was heated and had hot and cold running water in the bathrooms. Subsequently, the interpreters moved into the suburbs of Nuremberg, some near Fürth; most French personnel moved into the Zirndorf suburb, which was cordoned off with a guard stationed at the entrance to the compound. Four people lived together in a house, sometimes in double rooms. Colonel Dostert had a nice house with a yard in *Bülowstrasse 14*, where he lived together with officers of his staff, including Joachim von Zastrow, Peter Uiberall and his wife Erna, Alfred Steer and Sigmund Roth. The houses were mostly very comfortable and well-kept, but some of the interpreters felt it was unpleasant and unjust to live in houses whose owners had been thrown out.[16] Interpreters used a pool of motor vehicles for transportation to and from the courtroom,[17] or a free bus service during the day and free taxi service in the night.

Most of the houses had a housekeeper available for cleaning and food preparation, although meals were usually taken at the U.S.-run cafeteria in the courtroom, or at the Grand Hotel, which had a bar and the only restaurant for court personnel. Lunch in the courtroom was not a culinary thrill, and it often consisted of bologna sandwiches. "The cafeteria supplied the noonday meal on weekdays for all persons in the courthouse, except guards, who were fed at their units. Prices were three Marks (thirty cents) for civilians, one Mark for officers, and free for enlisted personnel of all the nations, and visitors."[18] Food was better at the Grand Hotel, where Spam and powdered eggs were served, all imported from the United States. Americans were not allowed to give Germans occupation dollars, so they would leave a cigarette on the table as a tip.

Mr. Steer and other officers living with him "adopted" one air-raid shelter group, and secretly supplied food and shelter for the winter, although they were not allowed to.[19] There was a lot of suffering in the destroyed city, and, of course, interpreters were not indifferent to human tragedy.

Social Life

It is surprising that court personnel managed to have fun in Nuremberg. The gloomy atmosphere of the courtroom and the intense suffering of the city could make one think that no one at the time wanted to have fun. And yet, night life in Nuremberg was very active for court personnel, and the young army soldiers and young lawyers enjoyed the company of women court reporters and interpreters. Marie-France Skuncke, who was 20 at the time, remembers having a great deal of fun, though in a frantic way, for a desperate need to escape from the gloominess of the courtroom.[20]

The "Grand," as the Grand Hotel was called, was also the only meeting point for court personnel during the night, "an isolated island of safety and entertainment."[21] Members of all nations would gather there to relax, play cards and drink at the bar; every night there was a dance of "thin, overpainted, half-starved German girls, not very young any longer,"[22] or some "vaudeville performances of tumblers and jugglers."[23] Interpreters could also participate in arranged trips, such as visits to Munich and ski weekends in Garmisch and Berchtesgaden. Other sources of entertainment were the opera, hunting weekends and the frequent parties and official dinners, where the interpreters would be present to ensure communication among the participants. At one of these, an embarrassing "interpreting" incident happened. It was a dinner at the Russian Prosecutor Rudenko's, organized in honor of Mr. Vyshinsky, later Soviet Deputy Foreign Minister and delegate to the United Nations. At this dinner, after innumerable toasts and drinks, Vyshinsky proposed a toast to the death of all the defendants. The court members of the Western delegations drank without waiting for the translation of the interpreter.[24] When they realized what had been said, there was concern that this would affect the credibility of the fairness of the trial. In the end, the incident had no consequences except for some bad consciences. It did not happen very often, however, that court personnel was invited to Russian parties. It is reported that the

> Russians lived in their requisitioned houses literally behind barbed wire. Sounds of singing, music, revolver shots in the night suggested that they held parties but no one was asked to them.[25]

Interpreters from the Western delegations resented the segregation in which Russian personnel were kept. They were not allowed to get in closer contact with the Russians. For this reason, while Mr. Steer and Uiberall were able to provide the addresses of many U.S., French and British interpreters, no one has detailed information about the Russian interpreters, apart from the names of some of them. The AIIC (International Association of Conference Interpreters) unsuccessfully tried to get in touch with Russian interpreters for the video they produced in 1992 on Nuremberg interpretation.

Relationships among Interpreters and with the Court

The close contact in the courtroom and during the evenings created lifelong friendships among interpreters. Many of them shared an interest in foreign languages and cultures; they also shared two or more languages and could socialize easily. Their relationship with the court was also good, and they even inspired admiration in some of the defendants.

As the American interpreters saw it, within the Western delegations, relations were good and interpreters got along well. The French were very cooperative and friendly and the British provided the most qualified, high-caliber personnel, for whom the Americans had a great respect. They all admired Wolfe Frank from Great Britain, who was unanimously seen as the best interpreter.

Relations with the Russians were different. Because of the segregation to which the Russian personnel were subjected, relations between Western and Eastern delegations were sometimes difficult. The Americans viewed the Russians as difficult to work with, except for the women, most of whom were attractive and sociable. All the interpreters at the Russian desk were Soviets and the majority were women (six interpreters out of nine). They apparently had strict orders not to fraternize with Westerners,[26] which was almost impossible, considering that they worked closely together in the same courtroom. They were strictly supervised by

> the representative of the N.K.V.D. at Nürnberg (People's Commissariat of Internal Affairs—the secret police), who stalked joylessly about the corridors in ill-fitting incognito, his dour eye on citizens of the Union of Soviet Socialist Republics.[27]

He reported all the Soviet team members whom he discovered enjoying their time in the company of people from the West. Thus the Soviets who were most friendly and most easily fraternized with other delegations' members were suddenly sent home.

For example, a talented and pretty Russian interpreter named Tania, married to a Russian brigadier in Moscow, was sent home after she had attracted the attention of a young American officer. "She spoke slangy American, read *Life* and *Newsweek*, adored American movies... and dressed and danced to perfection... Doubtless she was having a good time, and had been so reported."[28] Oleg Troyanovsky, one of the best Russian interpreters, also enjoyed the company of Western colleagues and members of the tribunal. He was the son of a former Soviet Ambassador to the United States, had gone to school in America and spoke perfect English. He was usually friendly and talkative, but would become stiff and suddenly leave when "their KGB watchdog"[29] was around. Mr. Troyanovsky, too, had to leave soon and was sent to work at a conference of ministers in Paris.[30] Thus, because of the surveillance, relationships with the Russians were best on a one-to-one basis; when two or more of them were present, the situation usually became stiff. The Russian representative also reported people who overin-dulged in alcohol at the Grand Hotel bar.

Many interpreters inside the booth, regardless of nationality, used to help each other and work with team spirit. It is reported that Doris de Keyserlingh one day volunteered to replace John Albert for 10 to 15 minutes while he was finishing the translation of a document. On another occasion, the Russian-German translator was caught by a coughing spell, and the English into German interpreter sitting next to him tuned his headphones to the English translation and retranslated the English version into German, until his colleague could start inter-preting again.[31]

As for the interpreters' relationship with the court, it was gener-ally good. The only exception to this was the feeling that some shared within the Translation Division. Some resentment grew against the interpreters because of the fact that only a few were chosen for the job, and because they were seemingly working fewer hours than other lan-guage personnel. Someone who had been rejected for the interpreting position would remark sourly: "Oh, I would not like to sit behind that glass partition like a monkey in a cage!"[32] Defense or prosecution law-yers occasionally criticized the interpreting system or the interpreters' versions, but on the whole relations were friendly. They sometimes approached the booths to have a clarification on a term or expression they did not understand. The interpreters especially liked the Presiding Judge Lawrence, whom they considered the savior of the interpreters.[33] He showed a deep understanding and appreciation for their problems and difficulties, and constantly reminded the speakers to "look for the light." Peter Uiberall recalls a funny episode about interpreters and Lord Justice Lawrence, which shows their amicable relationship:

> One day, I remember, he seemed to doze off... the German-English interpreter lowered his voice and then SUDDENLY SPOKE LOUD. We could see Lawrence's head bob up, and we smiled at each other.[34]

Among the defendants, some had a special relationship with the interpreters. While at the beginning some of them seemed to sneer at the whole set-up of simultaneous interpreting,[35] many soon realized that the system was efficient and that the interpreters were working hard for them to understand the proceedings. The defendant Albert Speer, fluent in English and French, was fascinated by the system and was the first to show interest in its mechanics. Uiberall, monitor and interpreter, dubbed him the interpreters' assistant because he was able to judge whether people were suited for the interpreting task. When Steer, then Head of the Interpreting Branch, put a new recruit in the booth, Speer would tune in and listen for a few minutes to the new interpreter. Then he would look over to the monitor and give his judgement with a nod yes or a shake no. The astonishing thing was that he was right every time.[36] Hjalmar Schacht, too, was fluent in English, because he had been brought up in Brooklyn; he and Speer were the interpreters' favorites: when they heard the interpreter stuck on a difficult German word or expression, one of them would write the translation on a piece of paper, and pass it along the dock until it was slipped under the interpreters' glass panel.[37] Both of them had understood the importance of good translation for themselves, and tried to help as much as they could.

Other defendants understood that cooperation with interpreters was in their interest. Alfred Jodl noticed that the interpreters worked more efficiently when they had the written text in front of them. He contacted Steer and asked him for permission to supply the text of his final plea beforehand and have it pretranslated. In this way, he both facilitated the task of the interpreters and at the same time ensured that his speech received the best translation.[38]

Finally, Fritzsche had the greatest admiration for interpreters.[39] He usually sat next to the glass partition and had the chance to observe them at work. He describes the interpreting system to some length in his memoirs and describes his understanding for their efforts and difficulties. As mentioned earlier, he even compiled a list of "Suggestions for Speakers" to facilitate their task.

It is astonishing to learn about this friendly relationship between interpreters and some defendants, and about the complicity among them on linguistic matters. Interpreters were probably the only people in the courtroom who treated the defendants like human beings and accepted their help and suggestions. As Speer reports in his memoirs:

> In the courtroom however we encountered only hostile faces, icy dogmas. The only exception was the interpreters' booth. From there I might expect a friendly nod.[40]

The relationship that grew across the front glass panel is not necessarily disturbing. Interpreters were not there to accuse or judge; it was not their job. They were providing a specific service: to ensure communication between groups speaking different languages. And that required cooperation and intercourse with the speakers, including the defendants. Of course, it must have been a striking contrast for interpreters to establish good relationships with some of the defendants and at the same time hear about the atrocities committed by them as Nazis. It was probably difficult to identify those "twelve broken men,"[41] to whom they could relate, with the major Nazi criminals referred to by the prosecution. But the defendants were on trial, and therefore were innocent until proved guilty. In the end, the two most cooperative defendants, Fritzsche and Schacht, were acquitted of those crimes and set free.

Notes

1. The U.S. was the host nation because Nuremberg was in the American zone of occupation.
2. Charles A. Horsky, "Memorandum for Mr. Justice Jackson" (ts. Sept. 5, 1945).
3. Robert J. Gill to John W. Griggs, U.S. Office of Chief of Counsel, "Re: Personnel for Interpreting and Translating Division," letter (ts. Sept. 26, 1945).
4. Alfred G. Steer, letter to the author (Feb. 14, 1995).
5. Frederick C. Treidell, letter to the author (May 2, 1996).
6. Siegfried Ramler, letter to the author (Feb. 1, 1995).
7. Frederick C. Treidell, letter to the author (May 2, 1996).
8. A PX (Post Exchange) is a shop at a U.S. military base.
9. Elisabeth Heyward, interview (AIIC, *Nurnberg*, Geneva 1992, videocassette).
10. Ann and John Tusa, *The Nuremberg Trial* (London: Macmillan, 1983): 124.
11. International Military Tribunal, Seventeenth Organizational Meeting (ts. Oct. 29, 1945).
12. Hilary Gaskin, ed., *Eyewitnesses at Nuremberg* (London: Arms, 1990): 69.
13. George Khlebnikov, interview (AIIC, *Nurnberg*, Geneva 1992, videocassette).
14. The document from which this information is drawn, "Current Translating Division Personnel List," bears no date, but Mr. Steer estimates that it was drafted during the spring of 1946.
15. Alfred G. Steer, "Interesting Times: Memoir of Service in U.S. Navy, 1941-1947" (ts. 1992): 290.
16. Alfred G. Steer, "Interesting Times: Memoir of Service in U.S. Navy, 1941-1947" (ts. 1992): 235.
17. *The Nuremberg Trial.* Photographs by Charles A. Alexander (ts. n.d.): page 1 of the captions.
18. *The Nuremberg Trial.* Photographs by Charles A. Alexander (ts. n.d.): page 5 of the captions.
19. Alfred G. Steer, letter to the author (April 22,1995).
20. Marie-France Skuncke, interview (AIIC, *Nurnberg*, Geneva 1992, videocassette).
21. Ann and John Tusa, *The Nuremberg Trial* (London: Macmillan, 1983): 228.
22. Francis Biddle, *In Brief Authority* (Garden City: Doubleday, 1962): 377.
23. Francis Biddle, *In Brief Authority* (Garden City: Doubleday, 1962): 377.
24. Montgomery H. Hyde, *Lord Justice: The Life and Times of Lord Birkett of Ulverston* (New York: Random, 1964): 501.
25. Ann and John Tusa, *The Nuremberg Trial* (London: Macmillan, 1983): 231.
26. Alfred G. Steer, letter to the author (Feb. 14, 1995).

27. Francis Biddle, *In Brief Authority* (Garden City: Doubleday, 1962): 377.

28. Francis Biddle, *In Brief Authority* (Garden City: Doubleday, 1962): 377.

29. E. Peter Uiberall, "Court Interpreting at the Nuremberg Trial" (ts. April 11, 1995): 2.

30. Francis Biddle, *In Brief Authority* (Garden City: Doubleday, 1962): 377.

31. "Information Concerning Interpreters" (ts. Spring 1946: 3).

32. E. Peter Uiberall, "Court Interpreting at the Nuremberg Trial" (ts. April 11, 1995): 2.

33. Hilary Gaskin, ed., *Eyewitnesses at Nuremberg* (London: Arms, 1990): 85.

34. Hilary Gaskin, ed., *Eyewitnesses at Nuremberg* (London: Arms, 1990): 85.

35. Alfred G. Steer, "Interesting Times: Memoir of Service in U.S. Navy, 1941-1947" (ts. 1992): 248.

36. Alfred G. Steer, "Interesting Times: Memoir of Service in U.S. Navy, 1941-1947" (ts. 1992): 248.

37. Hilary Gaskin, ed., *Eyewitnesses at Nuremberg* (London: Arms, 1990): 84.

38. Alfred G. Steer, "Interesting Times: Memoir of Service in U.S. Navy, 1941-1947" (ts. 1992): 250.

39. Hans Fritzsche, *The Sword in the Scales: As Told to Hildegard Springer.* Trans. by D. Pyke and H. Fraenkel (London: Wingate, 1953): 81.

40. Albert Speer, *Inside the Third Reich: Memoirs by Albert Speer.* Trans. by Richard and Clara Winston (London: Macmillan, 1970): 608.

41. Robert H. Jackson, *The Case against Nazi War Criminals: Opening Statement for the United States of America by Robert H. Jackson and Other Documents* (New York: Knopf, 1946).

CHAPTER FIVE

PROFILES OF INTERPRETERS

The interpreters of the Nuremberg Trial were generally well-educated and intelligent people. They came from different countries and their educational and professional experience was diverse: there were college professors, lawyers, medical people, graduate students, radio broadcasters, army officers and professional interpreters. "Displaying much individuality, they were heard and seen more than anyone else in the courtroom."[1] Most of them were occasional interpreters who did not continue the profession afterwards and went back to their jobs.[2] Their different origins, careers and endeavors before and after the trial are reflected in their extremely varied biographical sketches presented in this chapter, which attempt to provide the following information: origins and languages spoken; schooling and education; recruiting and training for the trial, and post-trial occupations. The list is incomplete; since most information has been supplied by Americans, it contains mainly files about U.S. interpreters. There are some files about French interpreters and Russian émigrés, while information about most British and Soviet interpreters is missing. The order of presentation is alphabetical, except for Léon Dostert, the first Head of the Translation Division.

Léon Dostert

Léon Dostert was Head of the Translation Division and the first Chief Interpreter at Nuremberg. It was his idea to introduce simultaneous interpretation at the Nuremberg Trial. He was born in 1904 in France and studied German and English at an early age.[3] He served as interpreter both for the German Army, occupying his town during the First World War and for the American Army which liberated it. In 1921 he moved to California and then to Georgetown University, in Washington, D.C., where he received his B.A. and M.A. from the School of Foreign Service. During his time at Georgetown he taught French, and by 1939, after completing his Ph.D., he was Professor of French and Chairman of the Department. He was called by the State Department to act as interpreter in numerous international conferences in Europe. He became an American citizen in 1941 and soon after enlisted in the American Army to fight in Europe, where he became, in 1944, French interpreter of General Dwight Eisenhower. In 1945, then an Army Colonel, he was in charge of organizing simultaneous interpretation at the Nuremberg Trial, and in 1946 he was called to organize the same system at the United Nations. Together with Reverend Walsh, he founded the Institute of Languages and Linguistics at Georgetown University (1949), of which he was director until 1959. Under his direction, the Institute pioneered the use of linguistic laboratories and instituted English centers in foreign countries. Starting in 1953 he collaborated with IBM on an experiment with machine translation, a project that grew rapidly both in the U.S. and abroad. In 1960, Professor Dostert also initiated a program to train blind people to learn and teach languages. Léon Dostert died in September 1971 in Bucharest, where he was attending a conference.

Dostert is generally recognized as the person who introduced simultaneous interpretation to Nuremberg and to the United Nations. At the IMT trial he worked as a French into English interpreter and often acted as a monitor. Considered a hard master, and temperamental, he imposed high standards of linguistic proficiency and required complete dedication to the job. The high level of performance attained at the trial was due to a large extent to his commitment. Not everyone liked him, though. Alfred Steer, his deputy, thought he was a difficult man to work with, and he used to push the execution of his good ideas on subordinates.[4] His critics named him "le Petit Napoléon," and Mr. Uiberall believes that, considering what he accomplished, he probably lived up to that title.[5] Dostert was also ready to defend his staff, as happened on the day when Justice Jackson, the American Prosecutor, claimed he had been given a wrong translation of an important document.[6] When Jackson complained to Dostert about the translation, the latter defended his staff saying that the translation had not changed the meaning of the text. In general, Dostert was considered a brilliant and able man and an inspiring leader, and the interpreting profession owes him a great deal.

His writings and publications include:

"The Instantaneous Multi-Lingual Interpreting System in the International Military Tribunal." Ts. n.d. Box 15. Francis Biddle Papers. Syracuse University.

France and the War.   New York: Oxford University Press, 1942.

"People Speaking to People." University of Chicago Roundtable Transcripts of Radio Program 821. Jan. 3, 1954. Chicago: University of Chicago, 1954.

Ed. *Research in Machine Translation.*   University of Georgetown Monograph Series on Language and Linguistics 10. Report of the 8th Annual Roundtable Meeting on Linguistics and Language Studies. Washington, D.C.: The Institute of Language and Linguistics, Georgetown University, 1957.

John Albert

Mr. Albert worked at the Nuremberg Trial at the German desk. Before the war, he was forced to leave his legal practice in Vienna because of Nazi race discrimination, and emigrated to the U.S.[7] He worked as an interpreter during the pretrial interrogation of Keitel and other defendants.[8] He was a court interpreter for English into German, but did not stay longer than the first weeks of the trial. He came to Nuremberg from the U.S. Office of War Information and returned to New York, where he worked for the U.S. Information Agency.[9]

Boris B. Bogoslowski[10]

Boris Bogoslowski, an American citizen of Russian origin, briefly served as court interpreter in Nuremberg. Before the trial he had founded the Russian Language School near Boston, where he also worked as a teacher. In the first week of the trial, he was Uiberall's roommate at the Grand Hotel. A highly educated linguist, he was first hired as an interpreter. He reported for duty on October 31, 1945 and was given a base pay of $3,640, which was later raised to $3,970.[11] However, he did not stand the strain of simultaneous interpretation for long, probably partly because of his age (over 50) and his unfamiliarity with recent Russian terminology (he had fled Russia a long time before). He then continued to work in Nuremberg as a document translator.[12]

Margot Bortlin Brant

Margot Bortlin, originally from Milwaukee, Wisconsin, came to Nuremberg right after graduating from high school in Minneapolis.[13] She translated German into English at the IMT trial. Her nickname "Passionate Haystack," "known to all but herself,"[14] was due to her passionate interpreting. In the booth she spoke with great emphasis, smiling and frowning, with "sweeping gestures and dramatic vocal inflections,"[15] producing both admiration and amusement. "Haystack" refers to the complicated hairdo she invented for her rich, blond hair, in order to accommodate the metal band of the headphones. It was a towering hairdo, "magnificent to watch as she worked."[16] Margot Bortlin is listed on the Personnel List of the Translation Division as receiving a CAF-11 pay. She is also mentioned in an episode in the memoirs of the American Judge Biddle:

> at a dance where we met she seemed a little stiff and could say only "Yes, Judge," "Oh no, Judge," "You don't say, Judge," handling her glass with a stiff and polished little finger, almost at right angles, emphatically elegant. Thinking that it would be easier than conversation I asked her to dance. If her cheek to cheek was still formal we were at least on a level."[17]

Thomas K. Brown

Tom Brown, an American citizen, worked as court interpreter at Nuremberg at the German into English position. He came to Nuremberg as a civilian; he was a college instructor and lived in New York City. Before the trial he did some propaganda broadcasting to Germany for the OWI (Office of War Information).[18] He was hired as an interpreter on October 17, 1945 and given a base pay of $4,300. He was housed at the Grand Hotel and worked under the supervision of Léon Dostert. His Temporary Duty expired on April 17, 1946. He did not continue with interpreting afterwards and went back to teaching. Today Mr. Brown lives in Maryland.

Haakon Maurice Chevalier

Haakon Chevalier worked in Nuremberg at the beginning of the IMT Trial at the French into English position, and sometimes as English into French interpreter. He was one of the few experienced interpreters. He held dual nationality (French/American).[19] He received his Ph.D. in

Romance Languages in 1929 at the University of California at Berkeley, where he worked as a teacher of French. In 1944, he worked for the first time as an interpreter for the International Labor Organization in Philadelphia. In 1945, he was asked by the French government, through the French consulate in San Francisco, to work as a consecutive interpreter at the first meeting of the United Nations, which was going to be held from April to June 1945. Immediately after the end of the United Nations Conference on June 26, he was called by the War Department in Washington and asked to work as an interpreter at the War Crimes Trial in Nuremberg. In early September he received his assignment in Washington from the War Department and was given the rank of colonel; soon after he left California, where he lived, and was flown to Nuremberg. He reported to Nuremberg on October 20, 1945 and was hired as an interpreter with a base pay of $6,230. In Nuremberg he was put under the supervision of Léon Dostert and lived at *Gartensteig 1*. During his time in Nuremberg he worked as court interpreter and co-authored a glossary of legal terms together with Major Egbert and Captain MacIntosh. He later left Nuremberg with his colleague Mr. David McKee,[20] with whom he had come to Nuremberg, and returned to California in May 1946. He then joined Dostert at Lake Success to help him launch the simultaneous interpretation at the United Nations. The old guard of consecutive interpreters were fighting hard against the introduction of simultaneous interpretation; Chevalier felt he had to make his Nuremberg experience available to Dostert, in order to contribute to the success of the UN operation. Haakon Chevalier authored and translated numerous books. He was later accused by the FBI and CIA of spying on the work of his good friend J. Robert Oppenheimer, as he relates in his book *Oppenheimer: The Story of a Friendship*. Mr. Chevalier died a few years ago.[21]

The publications of Haakon Chevalier include:
"Anatole France." Ph.D. thesis. University of California at Berkeley, Dec. 12, 1929.
André Malraux and "Man's Fate" [La Condition Humaine]. New York: Smith, 1934.
For Us, the Living. New York: Knopf, 1948.
The Ironic Temper: Anatole France and His Time. New York: Oxford University Press, 1932.
The Last Voyage of the Schooner Rosamond. London: Deutsch, 1970.
The Man Who Would Be God. New York: Putnam, 1959.
Oppenheimer: The Story of a Friendship. New York: Braziller, 1965.
Trans. *The Bells of Basel.* By Louis Aragon. New York: Harcourt, 1936. Trans. of *Les Cloches de Bâle.*

Trans. *Hidden Faces*. By Salvador Dali. New York: Dial Press, 1944.
Trans. of *Rostos Ocultos*.

Trans. *Hiquily*. By Alain Jouffroy. Paris: Fall, 1962.

Trans. *Residential Quarter*. By Louis Aragon. New York: Harcourt, 1938. Trans. of *Les beaux quartiers*.

Trans. *The Secret Life of Salvador Dali*. By Salvador Dali. New York: Dial, 1942.

Edith Coliver (nee Simon)

Edith Simon, a naturalized American citizen, first served as German-English, English-German consecutive interpreter in the pretrial interrogations and then as a court interpreter at the beginning of the trial. She subsequently worked as research analyst, conducting interrogations of female members of indicted Nazi organizations.[22] Having heard of the trial through the newspapers, she applied to the U.S. War Department (now Defense Department). She was first interviewed in Washington, D.C. for the Nuremberg assignment by Colonel Mickey Marcus. She was tested and then hired by Colonel Dostert on October 19, 1945, under whose tutelage she had worked as a Spanish/French/English translator at the first UN Conference in San Francisco in 1945. As interpreter in the Section Interpretation-Interrogation at Nuremberg she received a base pay of $2,980, serving under the supervision of Alfred Booth.[23] She was trained there for simultaneous interpretation, especially in a vocabulary of military and governmental terms that were going to be used in the courtroom. She lived with three colleagues in a sequestered house at *Bülowstraße 59*. After the trial she maintained a lifelong friendship with Siegfried Ramler, also a Nuremberg interpreter. Mrs. Coliver now lives in California.

Wolfe Hugh Frank

Wolfe Frank was by unanimous judgement the best interpreter of the trial. Born in Germany, son of a Jewish BMW plant manager, he escaped to England in the late 1930s. "A handsome young Bavarian,"[24] he came to Nuremberg as officer of the British Army, where "he had passed up the safe language positions offered him and had volunteered for the commandos,"[25] for which he was highly decorated. He spoke English with an upper-class accent, and could move back and forth effortlessly between German and English, a performance that was achieved only by Paul Otto Schmidt, Hitler's interpreter.[26] Frank worked in Nuremberg as a pretrial interrogation interpreter in Keitel's and other interrogations.[27] He was then selected by Peter Uiberall for the courtroom, who accepted him for the German-English position, even though Frank's native language was German. Frank occasionally worked from English into German.

> His use of German and English was noticeably better than that of most native speakers. His voice and manner, the nuances of his vocabulary, the ability to convey the character of the person for whom he was translating were all outstanding.[28]

In compensation for his brilliant performance, Frank asked to interpret some of the crucial moments of the trial, like the final statements of the defendants into English and the judges' sentences on the defendants into German.

Frank became Chief of the Interpreting Branch of the Language Division (renamed from the Translation Division) during the first year of the Subsequent Proceedings (1946-1947). He returned to England in civilian clothes. Wolfe Hugh Frank died in England, in 1988, at age seventy-five.[29]

Elisabeth Heyward

Elisabeth Heyward, a French national, worked as court interpreter at the IMT trial at the English into French position.[30] Before the trial she worked at the Agence France Presse in Paris, where she was part of a group trying to pick news from overseas broadcasts to be used by Agence France Presse. Everyone in France was well aware of the forthcoming trials, which had been given extensive publicity by the media. When the Main Trial was already halfway through, one of her colleagues, who had been recruited for Nuremberg earlier, gave her name when a vacancy occurred. She was interviewed in Paris and flown to Nuremberg. On the day she arrived, she went into the visitors' gallery, and was astonished to see and hear simultaneous interpreting. She thought it was impossible that interpreters could translate simultaneously, a practice she had never seen before. Despite this fact, she received no training at all. In the courtroom the following day, she had to launch into simultaneous interpreting and, after overcoming the initial difficulty due to the unfamiliar technique and vocabulary, she found that simultaneous interpreting was feasible after all and that she could do it. When the trial was over, she worked as a freelance interpreter for some time and was eventually recruited as an interpreter at the United Nations Headquarters, where she worked until her retirement in December 1981. After that time she continued on and off to work there as a freelance interpreter. She gives an account of her experience as a Nuremberg simultaneous interpreter in the interview by AIIC.[31] Ms. Heyward now lives in New York.

Stefan F. Horn

Stefan Horn graduated from the School for Interpreters in Geneva and held a Doctorate in *rerum politicarum* from the University of Vienna.[32] In Geneva he had been trained as a consecutive interpreter. He applied to Nuremberg for an interpreter job and passed the test administered by a U.S. Army officer. He worked at Nuremberg as court interpreter (English into German) during part of the first trial and in the "Justice Case," and became Chief Interpreter. After the trials, in 1949, he joined Léon Dostert at Georgetown University, Washington, D.C.,[33] where he became Head of the Division of Interpretation and Translation of the Institute of Languages and Linguistics that Dostert had founded. He became an American citizen and lived in Maryland. He died August 9, 1996, age 96.[34] His publications include: *Glossary of Financial Terms in English/American, French, Spanish, German*. Amsterdam: Elsevier: 1965.

Armand Jacoubovitch

Mr. Jacoubovitch worked at Nuremberg as a court interpreter. He was a professional interpreter who graduated from the first Interpreters' School in Geneva. Mr. Jacoubovitch and his family had been in a concentration camp, from which he had miraculously managed to escape during the war. He worked for a couple of months as a simultaneous interpreter, then gave up and returned to the translation department.[35]

Patricia Jordan[36]

Patricia Jordan worked as a court interpreter at the IMT trial, covering the last four months of the Main Trial. She was brought up bilingually by English parents in Berlin until just days before the war broke out. After an interlude in London, spent mainly at the British Library, she joined her father in Switzerland, where she finished her schooling in Lausanne. By now a fluent French speaker, she obtained a degree in translation and conference interpreting (English/French/German) in six months at Geneva University. Shortly afterwards, Lieutenant Peter

Uiberall and Lieutenant Joachim von Zastrow, monitors at the Main Trial who were scouring the universities for new talent, tested her for simultaneous interpretation, a completely unknown technique to the would-be candidate. She was offered a year's contract and left right away for Nuremberg, at 21 years of age. Once there, she was reunited with five others recruited at Geneva University, including Frederick Treidell and Stefan Horn. Patricia Jordan is listed in the Nuremberg Personnel List as a British citizen hired as CWS-9 (Continental Wage Schedule).

Ms. Jordan was billeted at the Grand Hotel and remembers being paid a third of her salary at Nuremberg, the remaining two thirds being remitted to her bank account in Lausanne. After spending a week sitting in the courtroom to become familiar with the proceedings, she passed a test during a lunch break and was put in the English booth the following day, working from French into English. Her teammates were Virginia von Schon (German into English) and Jinka Paschkoff (Russian into English).

After the verdict, she was supposed to work in the German booth at the Subsequent Proceedings; however, the Chief Interpreter of UNESCO came looking for French-English interpreters for the new Paris-based organization. Patricia Jordan, together with Jean Meyer, Elisabeth Heyward and Marie-Rose Waller, left Nuremberg for UNESCO after being released from her contract.

She married a Belgian scientist and moved with him to Africa, working for several international organizations. She continued to work as an interpreter on returning to Europe, often teaming up with former Nuremberg colleagues, several of whom remained lifelong friends. She never left the profession, which she greatly enjoyed. Patricia Jordan now lives and still works in Brussels.

Klaus and Doris de Keyserlingh

Klaus de Keyserlingh, who interpreted French into German, was the only interpreter to sit side by side with his wife. Before the trial he worked as a corporate lawyer and practiced law in France, Germany and the United States.[37] Mrs. de Keyserlingh translated Russian into German and possibly also Russian into English. They were "among the original group of experienced conference interpreters brought to Nuremberg by Colonel Dostert, possibly "on loan" from U.S. government agencies and therefore not staying very long. Both were at least trilingual."[38]

George (Youri S.) Khlebnikov

George Khlebnikov, of White Russian origin, worked at the IMT Trial as interpreter for Russian into English, Russian into French and English into French. Born in 1923 in the Free City of Danzig, he spoke Russian, German, English and French. In 1945 he was 22 and was living in Paris. He had just graduated from the École des Hautes Études Commerciales. In December 1945, a French Foreign Ministry official called at his host's house looking for translators for Nuremberg. He and two other friends, who were also Russian émigrés, all spoke Russian, English and French. They decided to take the language test at the Hotel Majestic in Paris, which consisted of a translation of an English and a Russian text into French (their native language). They passed the test and took the train for Nuremberg on the next day. When they arrived late the next day in Nuremberg, they were brought into the empty courtroom, where Dostert asked them to interpret simultaneously a French, a Russian and an English text into either English or French. They doubted that it would be possible, because they had never heard of simultaneous interpreting, but tried. They passed this test too and started working in the booth the following day. George Khlebnikov was hired by the Americans with a base pay of $1,200, and given the rank of Colonel in the Army. He was registered as a Russian refugee and worked under the supervision of Joachim von Zastrow. He reported for duty on January 1, 1946 and his contract expired on August 10, 1946.

Mr. Khlebnikov left Nuremberg on August 13, 1946 for Paris and from there to the United States on August 16. He followed Dostert to the United Nations. He and other interpreters from Nuremberg (Rosoff, Vassiltchikov) had to show "old-guard" interpreters that simultaneous would work.[39] He was employed at the UN as an interpreter and became famous during the Cold War for his polished and cultured interpretations, first into French, later also into English. He was Chief of the Interpretation Service at the UN until his retirement in 1983, after which he continued to work as a freelance interpreter until 1996—a 50-year career which he started at the Nuremberg Trial.[40] George Khlebnikov died on his birthday in November 1996 in New York City.

C.D. MacIntosh

Mr. MacIntosh was a Scottish Captain who worked as a court interpreter at Nuremberg. He was one of the editors of the glossary of legal terms compiled by Haakon Chevalier and Major Egbert. He interpreted French into English but knew German as well as he knew French.

Jean Meyer

Jean Meyer, an officer in the French Army who served at Nuremberg in uniform with the rank of Commandant, worked as an interpreter of English into French, French into English and German into French.[41] He was one of the members of the staff who personally suffered from the Gestapo.[42] He was in charge of the interpreters of the French desk.[43]

Siegfried Ramler

Siegfried Ramler was a court interpreter during the IMT Trial and the Subsequent Proceedings; he then served as Chief of the Interpreting Branch in 1948 until 1949. He was born in Vienna in 1924.[44] He received his secondary education in London and his college education at the University of Paris. He received his M.A. degree from the University of Hawaii. During the war he was in London and worked, among other jobs, as a translator in governmental offices. Siegfried Ramler was selected to join the 9th United States Air Force Service Command in 1944, serving as language liaison officer in their advance into Germany. He was stationed in a city near Nuremberg, where the preparation for the trial was beginning. When he called the U.S. Office of Chief of Counsel in Nuremberg, which was responsible for recruiting personnel, he was asked to join the translating and interpreting staff. In Nuremberg, where he arrived before the beginning of the trial, he served as pretrial interrogator, which he considers the most interesting part of his experience in Nuremberg. He worked as a consecutive interpreter during Göring's pretrial interrogation, and also in the interrogations of von Ribbentrop, Keitel, Frank and Streicher.[45] When Dostert started to test people for the simultaneous interpretation, Mr. Ramler took the test and became court interpreter for German into English. He worked at the German into English position for the whole trial, acting sometimes as monitor, too. After the end of the Main Trial in mid-1946, he remained for the Subsequent Proceedings until 1949, and became the last Chief of the Interpreting Branch. Mr. Ramler is listed as a British national in the Personnel List, receiving a level-9 pay, which was later raised to CAF 11 (around $3,000 per year).

After the trials were over, he became Chairman of the Punahou Foreign Language Department, where he held other offices, too. Mr. Ramler has been founder and former president of numerous associations in Hawaii, such as the Alliance Française of Hawaii and the

Foundation for Study in Hawaii and Abroad. He has been lecturer of German, French and Political Science at the University of Hawaii, and was the Director of the Wo International Center at the Punahou School in Honolulu, until his retirement in 1995. He is currently a Visiting Fellow at the East-West Center in Honolulu and also serves as Chairman of the International Advisory Board of the Pacific Board Consortium.[46] Mr. Ramler now lives in Hawaii.

His publications include: "Origins and Challenges of Simultaneous Interpretation: The Nuremberg Trial Experience." American Translators Association. *Languages at Crossroads.* Ed. by Deanna Lindberg Hammond. Medford: Learned Information, 1988. 437-440.

Edouard Roditi

Edouard Roditi, a U.S. national, a writer and an academic, interpreted French into English in the first War Crimes Trial. Together with Haakon Chevalier, he was the only experienced interpreter of the staff, the only one who had worked with the IBM equipment before.[47] He always showed up in court in uniform. An art collector and art historian, he returned to Paris after the IMT trial.[48] He is listed on the U.S. payroll of the Translating Personnel List as receiving a P-5 pay.[49]

Genia (Evgenia) Rosoff

Genia Rosoff, a French citizen of Polish origin, was recruited to interpret Russian into French. Since she knew English, too, she sometimes worked from English into French.[50] Before the trial she lived in Paris, and worked as a newspaper woman. She was a member of the French underground. She came to Nuremberg as a survivor of the Ravensbruck Nazi concentration camp.[51] (Buchenwald according to "Information Concerning Interpreters.") Marie-France Skuncke remembers her as "one of the best interpreters I've ever met," and marvels at Genia Rosoff's performance in the courtroom despite the fact that she had suffered at the hands of the very Nazi criminals on the other side of the glass partition.[52] Genia Rosoff's title as a civilian was Professor. She was hired in Nuremberg as a court interpreter with a base pay of Fr 15,000, under the supervision of Léon Dostert. In Nuremberg she lived in *Vestner Straße 3* in the Zirndorf district. A "flaming redhead of Polish origins,"[53] she attracted Göring's attention continuously.

"One of the best of the French team,"[54] Genia Rosoff, together with Youri Khlebnikov and George Vassiltchikov, left on August 10,

1945 for Paris and then for New York, to start simultaneous interpretation at the United Nations.

Sigmund Roth

Sigmund Roth served in many offices at Nuremberg, including a period as Head of the interpreters. He was a highly decorated U.S. Army captain and had served for almost five years when he came to Nuremberg. He spoke German, Serbo-Croatian, some French and understood Russian. On November 9, 1945, he was recruited by Dostert and Steer, who hired him for their staff because of the paucity of personnel who could understand Eastern European languages. He first became the assistant Executive Officer of the Translation Division. Then he was employed as administrative Head of the court reporters (about 45 people) and of the reviewing branch (100 people). He offered invaluable help in the printing section, of which he became Director when the trials were half over. He remained to finish his printing job for more than a year after the trial had finished.[55] It is mostly thanks to his effort that the 43 volumes containing the transcripts of the proceedings and related documents were published after the trial in four languages. He came from New York City and in Nuremberg he lived at *Forsthaus Straße 36*. He was given a base pay of $175 a month. Sigmund Roth died in 1985, age 74.

Ignace Schilovsky

One of the Russian-English interpreters, Ignace Schilovsky was a former Czarist officer.[56] An American citizen, he came to Nuremberg as a civilian. He was hired as interpreter on October 30, 1945 at the pay of $3,640 a year. In Nuremberg he lived at *Uhland Straße 17*, apt. 6.

One day Alfred Steer, monitor, was told by the judges that some of the into-English interpreters had a strong accent and that it was tiring for the judges to listen to them. Steer took the heavily accented interpreters to the sound lab and showed them how to work with colleagues in order to improve their accents. One of these was Colonel Schilovsky, who later told Steer: "You know, Commanderr, that iss the first time I ever hearr I speak with haccent."[57]

Eugene S. Serebrenikov

Eugene Serebrenikov, a U.S. citizen, was a professional consecutive interpreter translating Russian into English. During the war, he acted as liaison officer with the Russians in Alaska, during the ferrying of planes from Alaska to Siberia.[58] He came to Nuremberg from California together with Haakon Chevalier and David McKee. He was hired on October 22, 1945 with the civilian grade CAF 10 at $3,920 per year. His supervisor was Joachim von Zastrow. In Nuremberg he lived at the *Lehrlingsheim* Hotel. He did not stay very long because he was not satisfied with simultaneous interpretation,[59] and left on July 1, 1946 for Berlin.

Marie-France Skuncke (nee Rosé)

Marie-France Skuncke, a French national from Paris, graduated in 1944 from the School of Interpreters in Geneva and had some experience in consecutive conference interpreting. She worked with the French occupation Army in Berlin and was recruited for Nuremberg for the French team, which was then pooled with the U.S. and British teams of the Interpreting Branch. When she arrived in Nuremberg in January 1946, she was 20 and had no experience of simultaneous interpreting. She spent the first two months in the training program, for which she was required to translate documents and perform special linguistic exercises during the mock trials. She also trained herself by sitting in the visitors' gallery and mentally translating the proceedings. In March 1946 she started working in the booth at the English into French position, even though she was trilingual (French/English/Polish). She was paid by the Americans, and her salary was much higher than what she received earlier from the French Ministry. Before going back to Paris she wrote an article in the scholarly journal *L'Interprète*, urging the introduction of simultaneous training at the Geneva School for Interpreters, which started to teach this technique soon afterwards.[60] She left Nuremberg after six months, because she had another contract. She continued with the interpreting profession and later became Secretary General of the International Association of Conference Interpreters (AIIC). In August 1992, she was invited to the Assembly of AIIC in Brussels, where she gave a lively account of her experience at Nuremberg.[61] Ms. Skuncke now lives in Paris. Her publications include: "Tout a commencé à Nuremberg." *Parallèles* 11 (1989): 5-8.

Harry N. Sperber

Harry Sperber was hired at Nuremberg as an interpreter of English into German. He was a U.S. Army captain and had served three and a half years before arriving in Nuremberg from New York City. Before the trial he had worked as broadcaster of sports events from the U.S. to Germany, and also had "the distinction of having attracted Goebbels' personal protests against his anti-Nazi broadcasts from America."[62] He had also compiled a German-English dictionary of military terms. In Nuremberg his supervisor was Léon Dostert. He reported for duty on November 16, 1945, and lived at the Grand Hotel. He left on July 8, 1946.

Alfred Gilbert Steer, Jr.

Mr. Steer was Deputy Chief and Executive Officer of the Translation Division, and became Head of the division after Dostert left for Lake Success in April 1946. Born in 1913 in the U.S., Steer received his M.A. degree from Duke University in 1938 and his Ph.D. degree in 1954 from the University of Pennsylvania.[63] In 1935-1936 he studied in Hitler's Germany as an exchange student. His main interest and subject of research as a scholar is Johann Wolfgang von Goethe and his age, as his many publications on the subject attest. "A gifted linguist,"[64] Mr. Steer was language educator at numerous universities, first as instructor, then as professor, and was the Head of the Germanic and Slavic Department at the University of Georgia from 1967 until he retired. In 1941-1947 he served in the U.S. Navy, in which he was eventually given the rank of Captain. He "spent the war skippering small ships in the Pacific"[65] and one ship he commanded in the Pacific was attacked by Japanese kamikaze aircraft.[66] During his service in the Navy he was recruited by Dostert as a linguist for the War Crimes Trials in Nuremberg, "his first shore duty in nearly four years."[67] When he arrived there he did not test out as an interpreter but became a valuable administrator (1945-1946). After his time in the Navy he returned to his previous profession of scholar and instructor. Mr. Steer was president of linguistic associations, such as the South Atlantic Modern Language Association, and director of programs, such as the Georgia Study Abroad Program and the Georgia Linguistics Program. Mr. Steer now lives in Georgia.

"An energetic amalgam of man of action and scholar,"[68] Alfred Steer had several duties when working for the Translation Division. As a start, he was in charge of recruiting the interpreters, and he was even sent across Europe to find them. His task was then to select interpreters and winnow out incompetent people. As Head of the Translation Division, he had to deal with defense counsel, who were pressing him for the translation of numerous documents, and had to explain that the division lacked funds, personnel and time. At the end of the trial, he was asked to translate the verdicts in advance and for reasons of security he organized a special group of translators who agreed to remain locked up for the duration of the translation.

Writings and publications of Mr. Steer include:

"Interesting Times: Memoir of Service in U.S. Navy, 1941-1947." Ts. 1992.

"Participation of Allied Delegations in the Work of the Translating Division." ts. July 30, 1946.

Goethe's Elective Affinities: The Robe of Nessus. Heidelberg: Winteruniversitätsverlag, 1990.

Goethe's Science in the Structure of the Wanderjahre. Athens: University of Georgia Press, 1979.

Goethe's Social Philosophy as Revealed in Campagne in Frankreich *and* Belagerung von Mainz. Chapel Hill: University of North Carolina Press, 1955.

Reading in Military Germany. With William W. Pusey, eds. Lexington: Edwards, 1942.

Ina Telberg

Mentioned in the Personnel List as a U.S. national, Ms. Telberg interpreted Russian into English during the Main Trial and was famous for speaking nine languages including some Japanese. She was a teacher at a girls' college before the trial. Afterwards, she published several reference books about Russia and Russian-English glossaries through her own publishing company in New York.

Ms. Telberg's publications include:

Russian-English Geographical Encyclopedia. New York: Telberg, 1960.

Russian-English Glossary of Psychiatric Terms. New York: Telberg, 1964.

Soviet-English Dictionary of Legal Terms and Concepts. New York: Telberg, 1961.

Who's Who in Soviet Science and Technology. New York: Telberg, 1960.

Who's Who in Soviet Social Sciences, Humanities, Art and Government. New York: Telberg, 1961.

Frederick C. Treidell

Fred Treidell, a French national, worked in the Nuremberg courtroom as court interpreter for German and French into English.[69] He studied Chemical Engineering, and learned English from his mother, and French and German from his father. Before the end of the Second

World War he took a crash course at the School for Interpreters in Geneva and received his diploma in Conference Interpreting in about seven months. A few days later, he was tested and hired by Joachim von Zastrow, one of Dostert's assistants, at Con-9 pay (Continental Wage Schedule), which was raised to CWS 11 a few months later. At Nuremberg, he became a close friend of Wolfe Frank, a fellow interpreter.

After leaving Nuremberg, Fred Treidell joined Tom Hodges (who had been Director of the Language Division of the U.S. Army at Nuremberg) to work for the American Administration of the Marshall Plan, with which he stayed until 1953. He then resumed his interpreting career, working as Chief Interpreter for the Western European Union, the European Productivity Agency, the World Veterans Federation and interpreting also for the OECD, ICAO, FAO, UNICEF and a number of non-governmental organizations. In 1962 he became Executive Secretary of AIIC (International Association of Conference Interpreters) and taught at the Interpreters' School of the Sorbonne University, Paris, from 1958 to 1964. In 1963 he was appointed President of the International Association of Chain Stores, and became a member of its board of directors after he retired in 1983. More recently, Mr. Treidell was appointed President of the Franco-American Association of Sister Cities, a position that he held for three years. Frederick Treidell lives in Paris.

Oleg A. Troyanovsky

Mentioned in Biddle's memoirs as the best Russian interpreter,[70] Oleg Troyanovsky was a bench interpreter at the Main Trial and spoke Russian, French, fluent English and probably also German. Son of the first Soviet Ambassador to the United States, he received his education in America. Before the trial he was recruited by the Soviet government to work as an interpreter and was present, for example, at the Meeting of Prosecutors in London in August 1945. He came to Nuremberg with the Soviet staff, and was kept under tight control by the Soviet representative:

> He had picked up American idioms, turns of humor, and ways of thinking, and seemed like an American boy, friendly and easy. We all liked him. I [Biddle] suppose it was conceived that he might be contaminated, for I can remember one evening, when three or four of us were lounging in a corner, laughing and gossiping, seeing him leap to his feet and leave the room as if he had suddenly remembered an engagement, when the N.K.V.D. [the secret police] man stalked by, pausing to frown for a split second. Troyanovsky left for a conference of ministers in Paris shortly afterward.[71]

Subsequently, he served as Nikita Krushchev's interpreter to the United States, and eventually became Soviet Ambassador to the United Nations.[72]

Ernest Peter Uiberall

Peter Uiberall was one of the interpreters who stayed longest at the trials. He worked there as monitor and interpreter from the beginning in 1945 and became Chief Interpreter during the Subsequent Proceedings, for which he remained in Nuremberg until 1948. He was born in Vienna in 1911 of a Jewish family, some of whose relatives were living in the United States.[73] He studied philology in Vienna, and in 1933-1934, as a Carnegie Endowment student lecturer, he traveled around the United States, talking to International Relations Clubs about the situation in Austria.

When Hitler occupied Austria in 1938, Uiberall and his wife, Erna, obtained a visa to the United States and left. In the United States he worked as a stock clerk in New York and as a farm laborer in Connecticut and New Jersey for three years. In 1944 he received American citizenship, and enlisted in the U.S. Army, where he became a second lieutenant in 1945. After the war he was serving in the U.S., while his wife, who had enlisted in the Women's Army Corps, was stationed near Frankfurt, in Germany, preparing material for the Nuremberg Trial. In Nuremberg the American delegation was looking for Americans who spoke German. When she mentioned that Mr. Uiberall's native language was German, they had him report to the Pentagon, where he met Colonel Dostert. On October 24, 1945 he was sent to Nuremberg. He first served as a document translator and staff officer of the Translation Division. As the trial started, he worked as monitor, and became court interpreter in February 1946 for German into English. During the Subsequent Proceedings he first worked as an assistant to the new director of the Language Division, then as a court interpreter and team chief in the "Justice Case" and finally as Chief of the Interpreting Branch and Acting Director of the Language Division in 1948. In that function, he had the job of phasing out the 300 people in the Language Division. After 1948 he returned to the Army and served another 18 years. He was assigned as an interpreter to the Headquarters of the U.S. forces in Austria (1951-1954), and for a few months he worked as interpreter at the U.S. Headquarters in Saigon, Vietnam. After retiring from the Army, he worked for eight years as Head of the translation section at the U.S. Air Force Headquarters in Washington, D.C.

Fred Treidell, interpreter, remembers Peter Uiberall as "a good friend and colleague."[74] He "worked reliably and dependably and cheerfully under all circumstances... He also had a fine sense of humor."[75] Apparently, he was quite popular among female Russian interpreters, and this provided a useful contact with the Russian contingent, considering that "cooperation with the Soviets [was] most difficult if not impossible."[76]

Writings of Mr. Uiberall include:
"Court Interpreting at the Nuremberg Trial." Ts. April 11, 1995.
"Simultaneous Interpreters at the Nuremberg Trial." Ts. July 25, 1995.

Benjamin Wald

Ben Wald was the other bench interpreter together with Oleg Troyanovsky, and could speak English, German, French and Russian. Sometimes he would help out at the Russian-English position. In Nuremberg he received a CAF-9 pay. A U.S. national, he came from Boston, Massachusetts.[77]

George Vassiltchikov

George Vassiltchikov was hired by the Nuremberg Translation Division to work as court interpreter for Russian into English and Russian into French. A former Lithuanian, before the trial he lived in Paris. He was hired on January 3-4, 1946. In Nuremberg his supervisor was Léon Dostert and he lived at the Grand Hotel. He was famous in Nuremberg for the fact that he stuttered in normal conversation but not when interpreting. He left Nuremberg on August 12, 1946 to fly to Paris in order to leave there on August 16 for New York City, where he started to work for the United Nations. He recently published the diary of his sister Marie ("Missie"), who lived in Nazi Germany as a Russian émigré, entitled *The Berlin Diaries: 1940-1945* (London: Chatto, 1985).

Other Interpreters

Margarete Abraham-Wagner, English into German.

Ursula Crowley-Prescott, German into English.

Leo Katz, English into German. Also worked as interpreter in the pretrial interrogation of Raeder and Frank.[78] He is listed on the Personnel List as a U.S. citizen receiving a CAF-6 pay.

Hans Lamm, English into German. Listed on the Nuremberg Personnel List as a U.S. citizen receiving a CAF-10 pay.

Helga Lund, German into English.

David McKee, French into English.

Helen Pashkoff (or Helene Paschkoff), French national, French into English.[79]

Hannah Schiller-Wartenberg, German into English.

Gerald Schwab, listed in the Personnel List as a U.S. citizen receiving a CAF-5 pay.

Lieutenant Tolstoy, Russian into French.

Ferdinand Wagner, English into German.[80]

Marie Rose Waller, who worked at the Main Trial for some months before returning to France.[81]

Mr. Mamedov, Ms. Kulakovskaya, Ms. Solovieva, Ms. Ninna Orlova (Secretary-Interpreter of Nikitchenko, the Russian Judge). Members of the Russian team, they interpreted into Russian from any other language. They were all at least trilingual.[82]

Notes

1. Telford Taylor, *Anatomy of the Nuremberg Trials: A Personal Memoir* (New York: Knopf, 1992): 228.
2. Marie-France Skuncke, Conference (AIIC, *Nurnberg*, Geneva 1992, videocassette).
3. Biography mainly based on Ross R. McDonald, "Léon Dostert." *Papers in Linguistics in Honor of Léon Dostert*. Ed. by William M. Austin (The Hague: Mouton, 1967).
4. Joseph E. Persico, *Nuremberg: Infamy on Trial* (New York: Viking-Penguin, 1994): 262.
5. E. Peter Uiberall, letter to the author (July 26, 1995).
6. The "mistranslation" accident is described in chapter 3 "Reliability and Impact of the Interpretation."
7. "Information Concerning Interpreters" (ts. Spring 1946): 2.
8. U.S. Office of Chief of Counsel for the Prosecution of Axis Criminality, *Nazi Conspiracy and Aggression* 2 (Washington, D.C.: Government Printing Office, 1948): 1381, 1521 and 1621.
9. E. Peter Uiberall, letter to the author (July 8, 1995).
10. The spelling of the name varies according to the source. This is the case with most of the Russian names, because of the different transliteration from the Cyrillic alphabet.
11. International Military Tribunal, "Personnel Index Card" (ms. and ts., Nuremberg, 1945-1946).

12. E. Peter Uiberall, letter to the author (Feb. 25, 1995).

13. Francis Biddle, *In Brief Authority* (Garden City: Doubleday, 1962): 398.

14. Telford Taylor, *Anatomy of the Nuremberg Trials: A Personal Memoir* (New York: Knopf, 1992): 229.

15. Telford Taylor, *Anatomy of the Nuremberg Trials: A Personal Memoir* (New York: Knopf, 1992): 229.

16. Francis Biddle, *In Brief Authority* (Garden City: Doubleday, 1962): 398.

17. Francis Biddle, *In Brief Authority* (Garden City: Doubleday, 1962): 398. Her picture appears on the cover of this book.

18. "Information Concerning Interpreters" (ts. Spring 1946): 2.

19. Haakon M. Chevalier, *Oppenheimer: The Story of a Friendship* (New York: Braziller, 1965): 84. Information on his life mainly taken from this text.

20. E. Peter Uiberall, letter to the author (Feb. 25, 1995).

21. AIIC, letter to the author (Feb. 17, 1995).

22. Edith Coliver, letter to the author (April 17, 1995).

23. International Military Tribunal, "Personnel Index Card" (ms. and ts., Nuremberg, 1945-1946). Alfred Booth was an interpreter in pretrial interrogations, such as Frank's and Raeder's. (U.S. Office Chief of Counsel for the Prosecution of Axis Criminality, *Nazi Conspiracy and Aggression* 2 [Washington, D.C.: Government Printing Office, 1948]: 1397, 1438.)

24. Telford Taylor, *Anatomy of the Nuremberg Trials: A Personal Memoir* (New York: Knopf, 1992): 229.

25. Joseph E. Persico, *Nuremberg: Infamy on Trial* (New York: Viking-Penguin, 1994): 269.

26. Joseph E. Persico, *Nuremberg: Infamy on Trial* (New York: Viking-Penguin, 1994): 263. For more information about Paul Otto Schmidt, see his book *Hitler's Interpreter*, ed. by R.H.C. Steed (London: Heinemann, 1950).

27. U.S. Office of Chief of Counsel for the Prosecution of Axis Criminality, *Nazi Conspiracy and Aggression* 2 (Washington, D.C.: Government Printing Office, 1948): 1311, 1316, 1641.

28. Ann and John Tusa, *The Nuremberg Trial* (London: Macmillan, 1983): 219.

29. E. Peter Uiberall, letter to the author (Feb. 25, 1995).

30. Elisabeth Heyward, letters to the author (April 14, 1995 and May 1, 1995).

31. AIIC (*Nurnberg*, Geneva 1992, videocassette).

32. Stefan F. Horn, letter to the author (Aug. 27, 1995).

33. E. Peter Uiberall, letter to the author (Feb. 25, 1995).

34. Nancy Horn, letter to the author (March 1997).

35. Marie-France Skuncke, AIIC Conference (AIIC, *Nurnberg,* Geneva 1992, videocassette).

36. This entry was written by Ms. Patricia Jordan, letter to the author (March 14, 1997) and slightly edited by the author.

37. "Information Concerning Interpreters" (ts. Spring 1946): 2.

38. E. Peter Uiberall, letter to the author (July 8, 1995).

39. George Khlebnikov, interview (AIIC, *Nurnberg*, Geneva 1992, videocassette).

40. United Nations, "George Khlebnikov (1923-1996)" 2.

41. E. Peter Uiberall, letter to the author (Feb. 11, 1995).

42. "Information Concerning Interpreters" (ts. Spring 1946): 3.

43. Marie-France Skuncke, AIIC conference (AIIC, *Nurnberg*, Geneva 1992, video-cassette).

44. Biographical information taken from his curriculum vitae and his letter to the author (Feb. 1, 1995).

45. U.S. Office of Chief of Counsel for the Prosecution of Axis Criminality, *Nazi Conspiracy and Aggression* 2 (Washington, D.C.: Government Printing Office, 1948): 1203, 1212, 1295, 1374-1384, 1426.

46. Siegfried Ramler, letter to the author (March 11, 1997).

47. Ann and John Tusa, *The Nuremberg Trial* (London: Macmillan, 1983): 218.

48. E. Peter Uiberall, letter to the author (Feb. 11, 1995).

49. "Current Translating Division Personnel List" (ts. Spring 1946).

50. Marie-France Skuncke, AIIC conference (AIIC, *Nurnberg*, Geneva 1992, video-cassette).

51. Dana A. Schmidt, "Pick Your Language." *The New York Times Magazine* 6 (Aug. 25, 1946): 24, and Francis Biddle, *In Brief Authority* (Garden City: Doubleday, 1962): 399.

52. AIIC, *The Interpreters: A Historical Perspective*, videocassette.

53. Dana A. Schmidt, "Pick Your Language." *The New York Times Magazine* 6 (Aug. 25 1946): 24.

54. E. Peter Uiberall, letter to the author (Feb. 25, 1995).

55. Alfred G. Steer, "Interesting Times: Memoir of Service in U.S. Navy, 1941-1947" (ts. 1992): 267.

56. Hilary Gaskin, ed., *Eyewitnesses at Nuremberg* (London: Arms, 1990): 40.

57. Hilary Gaskin, ed., *Eyewitnesses at Nuremberg* (London: Arms, 1990): 40.

58. "Information Concerning Interpreters" (ts. Spring 1946): 2.

59. E. Peter Uiberall, letter to the author (July 8, 1995).

60. Marie-France Skuncke, "Tout a commencé à Nuremberg." *Parallèles* 11 (1989): 7.

61. E. Peter Uiberall, letter to the author (Feb. 25, 1995).

62. Dana A. Schmidt, "Pick Your Language." *The New York Times Magazine* 6 (Aug. 25, 1946): 24, and "Information Concerning Interpreters" (ts. Spring 1946).

63. Biography based on "Steer, Alfred Gilbert, Jr." *Who's Who in America* (Chicago: Marquis Who's Who, 1991) and on his curriculum vitae.

64. Joseph E. Persico, *Nuremberg: Infamy on Trial* (New York: Viking-Penguin, 1994): 112.

65. "Information Concerning Interpreters" (ts. Spring 1946).

66. E. Peter Uiberall, letter to the author (Feb. 25, 1995).

67. "Information Concerning Interpreters" (ts. Spring 1946): 4.

68. Joseph E. Persico, *Nuremberg: Infamy on Trial* (New York: Viking-Penguin, 1994): 262.

69. All information taken from Frederick C. Treidell, letter to the author (Aug. 29, 1995).

70. Francis Biddle, *In Brief Authority* (Garden City: Doubleday, 1962): 377.

71. Francis Biddle, *In Brief Authority* (Garden City: Doubleday, 1962): 377.

72. E. Peter Uiberall, letter to the author (Feb. 25, 1995).

73. Biography based on Hilary Gaskin, ed., *Eyewitnesses at Nuremberg* (London: Arms, 1990), and E. Peter Uiberall, letter to the author (Feb. 11, 1995).

74. Frederick C. Treidell, letter to the author (Aug. 29, 1995).

75. Alfred G. Steer, letter to the author (Sept. 7, 1995).

76. Alfred G. Steer, letter to the author (Sept. 7, 1995).

77. E. Peter Uiberall, letter to the author (April 11, 1995).

78. U.S. Office of Chief of Counsel for the Prosecution of Axis Criminality, *Nazi Conspiracy and Aggression* 2 (Washington, D.C.: Government Printing Office, 1948): 1437, 1397.

79. Jinka Paschkoff, according to Ms. Jordan. She could be the same person or a relative.

80. These names are listed in E. Peter Uiberall, "Simultaneous Interpreters at the Nuremberg Trial" (ts. July 25, 1995).

81. Frederick C. Treidell, letter to the author (Feb. 5, 1997).

82. E. Peter Uiberall, letter to the author (Feb. 25, 1995).

CONCLUSION

On October 1, 1946, the trial came to an end. For many interpreters this meant a return to their previous profession; others stayed in Nuremberg for the Subsequent Proceedings. For some, Nuremberg was just the beginning of a new international career, as simultaneous interpreting spread around the world and more and more international organizations were created. Regardless of their successive careers, they witnessed and participated in one of the most important historical events of the twentieth century, revolutionized the field of interpretation and facilitated the organization of multilanguage conferences and the creation of international organizations. Certainly, something to be proud of. And yet, feelings are mixed and interpreters' opinions vary.

How do interpreters feel today about their Nuremberg experience? For some, Nuremberg was only a brief episode in their career. They have accomplished many other things in their lives that they consider more important. Usually, they do not remember many details about it. For others, the IMT trial was the starting point of their career, the place where they learnt to interpret simultaneously, and thanks to that they were able to work as freelance interpreters or work for organizations like the United Nations. For yet others, the IMT trial had a tremendous impact on their lives, because they worked there for a long time or because they had a personal reason to participate in the trials.

Frederick Treidell's main recollection about the IMT trial is the fact that simultaneous interpreting was so new and difficult. He also remembers that the general atmosphere of the trial was depressing, to the point that one became inured by all the atrocities.[1] Mr. Steer has an ambivalent view of his experience at Nuremberg. On the one hand, he feels he gave his contribution to an important event in history. *"Et quorum et ego pars minima fui"*[2] is the way he describes his Nuremberg experience, adapting the quote from Virgil and Goethe. On the other hand, Steer considers it an unpleasant experience, because of the intense suffering of the war-destroyed city, with the stench of rotting corpses still in the air. Also considering the subject matter dealt with in court, it was nothing but a "dirty job,... like many other dirty jobs, it had to be done."[3] He refers to the psychological torture of being exposed every day to an unparalleled degradation of human beings and of witnessing the atrocities and depravities in the Nazi camps. He writes in his memoirs:

> I shall never forget the words of one translator, working on the death-record books of one minor Nazi concentration camp. His voice shook as he realized with horror the full implications of what he was saying: "Those people died in alphabetical order!"[4]

The horror did not stop once interpreters left the courtroom. They were living in a city of intense misery and suffering, in houses whose owners had been thrown out, where the Germans were hungry and indolent because of their poor diet. Mr. Steer also condemns those of the U.S. personnel who let down their moral standards and took up with live-in girlfriends, even though they were married and had children back in the United States. He was not the only person to believe this, as this quotation from an article of the time shows:

> The necessary dependence on interpreters, the striking number of higher-rank officers in residence with mistresses, of vanished Nazi big wigs, the general air of maladroitness and cumbersome effort had given rise to a bitter description... The U.S. occupation rule of Germany and Austria was being called "the government of interpreters and mistresses."[5]

This whole atmosphere of degradation made people want to leave as soon as they had the chance, and the turnover rate for language personnel during the year of the trial exceeded 100 percent. The motivation was disgust, and the sense that they could be doing something as useful but more pleasant. The recurring thought was

> There are other more pleasant places I could go, other, more useful jobs I could do, without being forced all day every day to come face to face with such horrors. I give up! I quit! I'm going home![6]

And yet, despite all the unpleasant aspects of the job, Alfred Steer cannot deny that interpreters were also fascinated by the grandeur of the Main War Crimes Trial. He is aware that he was part of an event that had a major impact on twentieth-century history. Peter Uiberall is proud of his work at Nuremberg,[7] because he feels that interpretation had a key role in ensuring a fair trial to the defendants. He feels that the Nuremberg achievement was one of the most important things he ever did. He was able more than others to witness the use and development of the interpreting system in Nuremberg, because he arrived at the very beginning, when the system was still in its experimental stage, and helped to perfect it, remaining to use it till the very end of the trials.[8]

George Khlebnikov remembers that there was a lot of enthusiasm, especially among the youngest interpreters. They had the feeling they were doing something new and unknown, they were breaking new ground. They were proud to show to the whole world that simultaneous interpretation was feasible. They felt like pioneers, and were united by a deep team spirit. He also feels that the introduction of simultaneous interpretation to the UN was a great achievement, because it considerably improved the communication among delegations.[9]

Undoubtedly, despite the unpleasantness of the Nuremberg situation, the achievements of the Nuremberg interpreters are impressive: they made possible one of the most crucial trials of the century, contributing to its conduct and promptness; they created a new profession, and went on to introduce it and teach it around the world, thus facilitating the creation of international organizations and the understanding among delegates of all countries.

Notes

1. Frederick C. Treidell, letter to the author (Aug. 29, 1995).

2. Alfred G. Steer, "Interesting Times: Memoir of Service in U.S. Navy, 1941-1947" (ts. 1992): 311. "And of these things I too was a small part." Steer's translation.

3. Alfred G. Steer, "Interesting Times: Memoir of Service in U.S. Navy, 1941-1947" (ts. 1992): 231.

4. Alfred G. Steer, letter to the author (Apr. 7, 1995). The translator was probably translating a document like the official report from Mauthausen, a grotesque example of cynicism of the Nazi officials. The report noted that on one day in March 1945 "203 people had died at regular intervals, all of heart attacks and in alphabetical order." (Ann and John Tusa, *The Nuremberg Trial* [London: Macmillan, 1983]: 167.)

5. "Germany: Interpreters and Mistresses." *Time* (Oct. 15, 1945): 30.

6. Alfred G. Steer, letter to the author (April 7, 1995).

7. Hilary Gaskin, ed., *Eyewitnesses at Nuremberg* (London: Arms, 1990): 117.

8. Hilary Gaskin, ed., *Eyewitnesses at Nuremberg* (London: Arms, 1990): 149.

9. George Khlebnikov, interview (AIIC, *Nurnberg,* Geneva 1992, videocassette).

INTERPRETING AFTER THE TRIAL

As a result of its use at Nuremberg, simultaneous interpretation spread to the United Nations in New York and to every major international conference. Dostert was instrumental for its success at Nuremberg and supervised the installation of the interpreting system at the UN; he was responsible for the collaboration with IBM, who elaborated and improved the equipment; and he founded the School of Language and Linguistics at Georgetown University with a Division of Interpretation and Translation. His commitment to the use and spread of simultaneous interpretation was as strong after the trial as it was before.

On April 15, 1946, while the IMT trial was still going on and simultaneous interpretation was well established there, Léon Dostert was invited to go to Lake Success, New York, to introduce simultaneous interpretation to the United Nations. Until then, the UN had used consecutive interpretation. Unlike the IMT trial, consecutive interpreting was still feasible at the UN, because

> in spite of the rule laid down in the Charter, French and English were still the only two working languages, and Spanish and Chinese were not used. When Soviet delegates spoke in Russian, as they usually did, a member of their delegation, who was never a trained interpreter, translated what they had said into French or English, and the same person whispered to them a translation of what was said in French or English.[1]

Spanish was introduced as a working language during the drafting of the Constitution of the World Health Organization. The numerous Spanish-speaking delegations insisted that Spanish be used as a working language. Thus the problem of interpretation became more acute, because consecutive interpretation into two languages of the many long speeches considerably slowed down the proceedings. The situation finally became unbearable with the introduction of Chinese and Russian as working languages.

During the meeting of the first General Assembly in London at the beginning of 1946, the delegate from the Ukraine, Manouilsky, mentioned that at the concomitant Nuremberg Trial they were using a system of simultaneous interpretation. The UN, he said, should have the best delegates representing their countries and not those who are fluent in foreign languages. The proposal to introduce simultaneous interpretation at the UN was adopted by the General Assembly and a mission was sent to Nuremberg to see how the system worked.[2] After this, the UN invited Dostert to set up the same system for the United Nations. Thus, in early 1946, Dostert left Nuremberg with the certainty that simultaneous interpretation could work. Once he installed the system in New York, he negotiated a contract for 20 interpreters and four staff members including himself. He sent a telegram to Mark Priceman, telling him about the job and asking him to put together a team for the fall of 1946.[3] Dostert also invited some Nuremberg interpreters to join him. Mr. Chevalier joined him from California, where he had returned to teach after leaving Nuremberg. Directly from Nuremberg in August 1946 came Ms. Rosoff, Mr. Khlebnikov and Mr. Vassiltchikov. At the United Nations, just like at Nuremberg, Dostert held mock sessions to test and train interpreters, during which verbatim texts from earlier sessions were read to the interpreters. Once he had assembled a team of interpreters, he organized a demonstration to which he invited various personalities and UN delegates. At the demonstration session, as reported by the newspapers of the time, everything went wrong, from the microphones, which would not switch on, to the cables, which were not properly connected.[4] Maybe for this reason, at the UN simultaneous interpretation was not trusted wholeheartedly, especially at the beginning, because the delegates had no means of checking the accuracy of the translation. Therefore, for about a year, a consecutive interpretation was given after the speech had been delivered *and* translated simultaneously.[5] However, after some time, the delegates understood the advantage of simultaneous interpretation in terms of speed, and started vigorously asking for simultaneous interpreters. Teams were put together hastily to provide simultaneous interpretation to all the UN commissions.[6] In 1947 the UN held its first conference in which no consecutive interpretation was delivered at all.

Right after the Main Trial finished (October 1946), many of the interpreters with the right language combination left for the United Nations (French/Russian/English). They knew that their job at the trial was temporary, and that the Subsequent Proceedings would only be carried out in English and German. Thus while many English-German and German-English interpreters stayed in Nuremberg, because German was not a working language at the United Nations, many who spoke other languages left for New York, with the prospect of a long-lasting occupation.

The new recruits helped Dostert overcome the opposition of the old guard of UN consecutive interpreters, who considered it impossible (and for most of them it was) to hear and translate at the same time. Among these opponents were J.F. Rozan, Jean Herbert and especially André Kaminker, who had also opposed the introduction of simultaneous interpretation in Nuremberg.[7] They were contemptuous of simultaneous interpreters, whom they called "les téléphonistes."[8] For a time, rivalry between the two groups continued, but after Herbert and Kaminker left, Rabinowitch became Chief of both simultaneous and consecutive interpreters.[9] The new interpreters showed the old guard that their fears were unfounded. They demonstrated that after a regular training it was actually possible to translate simultaneously. Consecutive interpreters discovered that they could perform in the booth, and many "simultanéistes" learned the joys of consecutive interpretation. Right after simultaneous interpretation was introduced at the UN, it became necessary to hire a considerable number of new interpreters, especially as the number of working languages grew. The interpreting team of the United Nations soon acquired outstanding abilities in simultaneous interpretation.

Léon Dostert was instrumental in the installation of the simultaneous interpretation system at the UN and the collaboration with IBM, which once again volunteered to furnish the equipment and one-year servicing arrangement free of charge. Mr. Watson, then President of IBM, "set a policy whereby the equipment would be furnished on a non-profit, minimum charge arrangement that would allow its greatest use to all."[10] The interpreting equipment was installed in several rooms, like conference rooms and council halls. About 8,000 seats were equipped with headphones for the reception of five language channels. IBM soon discovered that the time and labor required to install the equipment was dragged out interminably by the need to wire all the microphones, headsets and speakers in the room. Not only was the installation long and expensive, it also created a "fixed" setting, that is, a setting in which people were not free to move around the room. To obviate this problem, IBM developed a complete wireless system. This system was first used "on a large scale at the International Radio Conference in Atlantic City in 1947."[11] With this system, the headphones were not connected to the tables, but to a battery-operated receiver with neck strap that the participant in the meeting could carry around. A total of 2,500 of these receivers were introduced soon after to the United Nations General Assembly.

Simultaneous interpreting quickly spread from Nuremberg to New York to every international conference. As a result, in the United States, interpreting became the most important function inside the Language Service Division of the U.S. government, while until then translation had been the main task of the Agency. This Agency, because of its small number of personnel, began to require that its interpreters work both simultaneously and consecutively from and into the languages they knew. This policy was not adopted by other organizations, which continued to require either consecutive or simultaneous from each interpreter and usually only required them to translate into their native language.

The spread of simultaneous translation since the end of the Nuremberg Trials has brought about the need for more simultaneous interpreters; increased mobility since the war has resulted in larger groups of potential interpreters. Both factors have brought about the birth of new Schools for Interpreters, and the introduction of simultaneous interpretation training at the School for Interpreters and Translators in Geneva. During the trial this was the only School for Interpreters in the world. It started teaching simultaneous interpretation on the suggestion of Marie-France Skuncke, Nuremberg interpreter, and its first two students in this discipline graduated in March 1952.[12] During that year the requirement "simultaneous interpreting" was added to the requirements for the completion of the *"diplôme de traducteur et interprète parlementaire"*[13] Other schools for interpreters were founded, after the Nuremberg Trial, such as the Division of Interpretation and Translation at Georgetown University created by Dostert. The growing importance of simultaneous interpretation has also brought about studies of interpretation and about its links with linguistics, psychology, language teaching, etc.[14]

It is interesting to note that simultaneous interpretation became known through the Nuremberg Trials, but it has since disappeared from courtrooms.[15] The most common mode of interpretation in courtrooms today is consecutive, partly because it does not require the installation of expensive simultaneous equipment, though it increases the length of the proceedings and thereby the cost of the trial. Still, from 1949 to today, a few trials have presented the same characteristics as the Nuremberg Trial, and they also dealt with the indictment of Nazi criminals (for example, the Eichmann and the

Demjanjuk trials of 1961 and 1987 respectively).[16] The linguistic confusion at the Demjanjuk trial shows once more what a remarkable job the Nuremberg staff was able to do, 42 years earlier and with rudimentary equipment.

Notes

1. Jean Herbert, "How Conference Interpretation Grew." *Language Interpretation and Communication*. Ed. by D. Gerver and Wallace H. Sinaiko (New York: Plenum, 1978): 7-8.

2. AIIC, *The Interpreters: A Historical Perspective*, videocassette. See also Ruth Morris, "Technology and the Worlds of Interpreting." In *Future and Communication: The Role of Scientific and Technical Communication and Translation in Technology Development and Transfer*. International Scholars Publications. Ed. by Y. Gitay and D. Porush (San Francisco: Rousenhouse, 1997): 177-184.

3. Mark Priceman, AIIC, *The Interpreters: A Historical Perspective*, videocassette.

4. AIIC, *The Interpreters: A Historical Perspective*, videocassette.

5. Jean Herbert, "How Conference Interpretation Grew." *Language Interpretation and Communication*. Ed. by D. Gerver and Wallace H. Sinaiko (New York: Plenum, 1978): 8.

6. AIIC, *The Interpreters: A Historical Perspective*, videocassette.

7. As described in Chapter 1 "Before the Trial."

8. "Telephone operators." My translation.

9. AIIC, *The Interpreters: A Historical Perspective*, videocassette.

10. A.C. Holt, "International Understanding: A Tribute to Mr. Thomas J. Watson" (ts. n.d.): 3-4.

11. "Language Barriers Broken by I.B.M. Simultaneous Interpretation System." *Audio Record* (December 1951): 5.

12. "Résultats des Examens pour l'obtention du diplôme." *L'Interprète* (March 1952): 13.

13. "École d'Interprètes de l'Université de Genève." *L'Interprète* (1952).

14. Interestingly enough, although simultaneous interpretation has spread and become common practice at conferences, sometimes delegates still do not understand its workings. Jean Herbert remembers that "Once, during a medical conference, a French doctor was evidently much intrigued by what we were doing, so he came and sat behind the booth while I was working with a colleague. At a time when we were silent, he seized the opportunity and asked us: 'Why are there two of you doing this work?' My colleague explained: 'We must. One of us listens and the other speaks.' The doctor was deeply impressed and passed on this valuable information to other delegates!" (Jean Herbert, "How Conference Interpretation Grew." *Language Interpretation and Communication*. Ed. by D. Gerver and Wallace H. Sinaiko [New York: Plenum, 1978]).

15. Ruth Morris, "Technology and the Worlds of Interpreting." In *Future and Communication: The Role of Scientific and Technical Communication and Translation in*

Technology Development and Transfer. International Scholars Publications. Ed. by Y. Gitay and D. Porush (San Francisco: Rousenhouse, 1997): 177-184.

16. See Ruth Lévy-Belowitz, "The Linguistic Logistics of the Demjanjuk Trial." *Parallèles* 11 (1989): 37-44, and Ruth Morris, "Eichmann vs. Demjanjuk: A Study of Interpreted Proceedings." *Parallèles* 11 (1989): 9-28.

APPENDIX

List of Court Members

From John A. Appleman, *Military Tribunals and International Crimes* (Indianapolis: Bobbs, 1954).

Counts, Verdicts and Sentences

From John and Ann Tusa, *The Nuremberg Trial* (London: Macmillan, 1983).

LIST OF COURT MEMBERS

Members and Alternate Members of the Tribunal

Lord Justice Lawrence, Member for the United Kingdom of Great Britain and Northern Ireland, President

Mr. Justice Birkett, Alternate Member

Mr. Francis Biddle, Member for the United States of America

Judge John J. Parker, Alternate Member

M. Le Professeur Donnedieu de Vabres, Member for the French Republic

M. Le Conseiller R. Falco, Alternate Member

Major General I.T. Nikitchenko, Member for the Union of Soviet Socialist Republics

Lieutenant Colonel A.F. Volchkov, Alternate Member

Prosecution

United States of America

Chief of Counsel:
Mr. Justice Robert H. Jackson

Executive Trial Counsel:
Colonel Robert G. Storey
Mr. Thomas J. Dodd

Associate Trial Counsel:
Mr. Sidney S. Alderman
Brigadier General Telford Taylor
Colonel John Harlan Amen

Assistant Trial Counsel:
Colonel Leonard Wheeler, Jr.
Lieutenant Colonel William H. Baldwin
Lieutenant Colonel Smith W. Brockhart, Jr.
Commander James Britt Donovan, U.S.N.R.
Major Frank B. Wallis
Major William F. Walsh
Major Warren F. Farr
Captain Samuel Harris
Captain Drexel A. Sprecher
Lieutenant Commander Whitney R. Harris, U.S.N.R.
Lieutenant Thomas F. Lambert, Jr., U.S.N.R.
Lieutenant Henry K. Atherton
Lieutenant Brady O. Bryson, U.S.N.R.
Lieutenant (j.g.) Bernard D. Meltzer, U.S.N.R.
Dr. Robert M. Kempner
Mr. Walter W. Brudno

United Kingdom of Great Britain and Northern Ireland

Chief Prosecutor:
H.M. Attorney-General, Sir Hartley Shawcross, K.C., M.P.

Deputy Chief Attorney:
The Rt. Hon. Sir David Maxwell-Fyfe, P.C., K.C., M.P.

Leading Counsel:
Mr. G.D. Roberts, K.C., O.B.E.

Junior Counsel:
Lieutenant Colonel J.M.G. Griffith-Jones, M.C.
Colonel H.J. Phillmore, O.B.E.
Major F. Elwyn Jones, M.P.
Major J. Harcourt Barrington

French Republic

Chief Prosecutor:
M. François de Menthon
M. Auguste Champetier de Ribes

Deputy Chief Prosecutor:
M. Charles Dubost
M. Edgar Fauré

Assistant Prosecutors (Chiefs of Sections):
M. Pierre Mounier
M. Charles Gerthoffer
M. Delphin Debenest

Assistant Prosecutors:
M. Jacques B. Herzog
M. Henry Delpech
M. Serge Fuster
M. Constant Quatre
M. Henri Monneray

Union of Soviet Socialist Republics

Chief Prosecutor:
General R.A. Rudenko

Deputy Chief Prosecutor:
Colonel Y.V. Pokrovsky

Assistant Prosecutors:
State Counsellor of Justice of the 2nd Class, L.R. Shenin
State Counsellor of Justice of the 2nd Class, M.Y. Raginsky
State Counsellor of Justice of the 3rd Class, N.D. Zorya
Chief Counsellor of Justice, L.N. Smirnov
Colonel D.S. Karev
Lieutenant Colonel J.A. Ozol
Captain V.V. Kuchin

Defense

Individual Defendants	Counsel
Hermann Wilhelm Göring	Dr. Otto Stahmer
Joachim von Ribbentrop	Dr. Fritz Sauter
	(to January 5, 1946)
	Dr. Martin Horn
	(from January 5, 1946)
Wilhelm Keitel	Dr. Otto Nolte
Ernst Kaltenbrunner	Dr. Kurt Kauffmann
Hans Frank	Dr. Alfred Seidl
Wilhelm Frick	Dr. Otto Pannenbecker
Alfred Rosenberg	Dr. Alfred Thoma
Julius Streicher	Dr. Hanns Marx
Fritz Sauckel	Dr. Robert Servatius
Alfred Jodl	Professor Dr. Franz Exner
	Professor Dr. Hermann Jahrreiss,
	Associate
Arthur Seyss-Inquart	Dr. Gustav Steinbauer
Martin Bormann, tried *in absentia*	Dr. Friedrich Bergold
Rudolf Hess	Dr. Gunther von Rohrscheidt
	(to February 5, 1946)
	Dr. Alfred Seidl
	(from February 5, 1946)
Walter Funk	Dr. Fritz Sauter
Erich Raeder	Dr. Walter Siemers
Baldur von Schirach	Dr. Fritz Sauter
Albert Speer	Dr. Hans Flachsner
Constantin von Neurath	Dr. Otto Freiherr von Ludinghausen
Karl Doenitz	Flottenrichter Otto Kranzbuehler
Hjalmar Schacht	Dr. Rudolf Dix
	Professor Dr. Herbert Kraus,
	Associate
Franz von Papen	Dr. Egon Kubuschok
Hans Fritzsche	Dr. Heinz Fritz
	Dr. Alfred Schilf, Associate

Groups and Organizations	Counsel
SS and SD	Ludwig Babel
	Horst Peleckmann
	Dr. Carl Haensel
	Dr. Hans Gawlik

SA	Georg Boehm
	Dr. Martin Loeffler
Gestapo	Dr. Rudolf Merkel
Leadership Corps of Nazi Party	Dr. Robert Servatius
Reich Cabinet	Dr. Egon Kubuschok
General Staff and High Command of the German Armed Forces	Dr. Hans Laternser

COUNTS, VERDICTS AND SENTENCES

Count 1: Conspiracy to Commit Crimes

Count 2: Planning, Preparing, Initiating or Waging Aggressive War

Count 3: Violations of the Law and Customs of War

Count 4: Crimes against Humanity

Defendant	Count 1	Count 2	Count 3	Count 4	Sentence
Hermann Göring	G*	G	G	G	Hanging
Rudolf Hess	G	G	I	I	Life
Joachim von Ribbentrop	G	G	G	G	Hanging
Wilhelm Keitel	G	G	G	G	Hanging
Ernst Kaltenbrunner	I	—	G	G	Hanging
Alfred Rosenberg	G	G	G	G	Hanging
Hans Frank	I	—	G	G	Hanging
Wilhelm Frick	I	G	G	G	Hanging
Julius Streicher	I	—	—	G	Hanging
Walter Funk	I	G	G	G	Life
Hjalmar Schacht	I	I	—	—	Acquitted
Karl Doenitz	I	G	G	—	10 years
Erich Raeder	G	G	G	—	Life
Baldur von Schirach	I	—	—	G	20 years
Fritz Sauckel	I	I	G	G	Hanging
Alfred Jodl	G	G	G	G	Hanging
Martin Bormann	I	—	G	G	Hanging
Franz von Papen	I	I	—	—	Acquitted
Arthur Seyss-Inquart	I	G	G	G	Hanging
Albert Speer	I	I	G	G	20 years
Constantin von Neurath	G	G	G	G	15 years
Hans Fritzsche	I	—	I	I	Acquitted

* G: guilty; I: innocent. Where there is no symbol in the table, the defendant was not charged.

BIBLIOGRAPHY

Unpublished Materials

Depositories

Bancroft Library, University of California at Berkeley.

    Chevalier, Haakon Maurice. Collected Reprints. 1931-1932.

    Gill, Virginia Tracy Hunter. Virginia Tracy Hunter Gill Papers [ca. 1945-1947]. Ms. MSS 83/108 Z. Portfolio.

National Archives, College Park, Maryland. National Archives Collection of World War Two Crimes Records, 1940-1948. 238.4 Photographs and lantern slides taken for the IMT at the U.S. Military Tribunals at Nürnberg, Germany. NT, NTA.

    The Nuremberg Trial. Photographs by Charles W. Alexander. 238 NTA.

National Archives, Washington, D.C. Jackson Papers. Record Group 238. Entry 51, box 39, folder "Translators." National Archives Collection of World War Two War Crimes Records, Records of the U.S. Counsel for the Prosecution of Axis Criminality, Main Office Files, 1945-1946.

    Anderson to William E. Jackson. Letter, ts. Aug. 8, 1945.

    Blake to Justice Jackson. Telegram 7100, ts. Aug. 22, 1945.

    Byrnes to Jackson. Telegram 7341, ts. Aug. 27, 1945.

    Calvocoressi, Peter to Justice Jackson. Letter, ts. Oct. 12, 1945.

    Gill for Jackson. Telegram 1128, ts. Sept. 22, 1945.

    Gill, Robert J. to John W. Griggs, U.S. Office of Chief of Counsel, Washington D.C. "Re: Personnel for Interpreting and Translating Division." Letter, ts. Sept. 26, 1945.

    Gill to Office CC Nurnberg Ensign Jackson. Telegram 1412267, ts. n.d.

    Horsky, Charles A. "Memorandum for Mr. Justice Jackson." Ts. Sept. 5, 1945.

    Horsky to William Jackson. Telegram 6966, ts. Aug. 17, 1945.

    Horsky to Justice Jackson. Telegram 7099, ts. Aug. 22, 1945.

International Business Machine Corporation. "That All Men May Understand." Ts. n.d.

"Interpreters." Ms. n.d.

Léon Dostert to R.J. Gill. Ts. Mar. 20, 1946.

"Record of Telephone Conference," ts. Oct. 1, 1945.

"Record of Telephone Conference," ts. Oct. 2, 1945.

U.S.FET Main AG 251720 to U.S. Chief of Counsel Nuremburg [sic]. Telegram S-25136, ts.

W. Jackson to the Secretary of State Byrnes. "Memorandum for Secretary Byrnes." Oct. 1, 1945. State Department Central Decimal files 1945-9. File No. 740.00116 EW Prosecution/10-145.

War Department to Office of Chief of Counsel, Nurnberg. Telegram 1322147, ts. Sept. 17, 1945.

Public Records Office, London. Foreign Office Documents. FO371 series.

Chief Prosecutors. Note of Meeting. Ts. FO371.51036. Aug. 31, 1945.

Report No. 3 of British War Crimes Executive. Ts. FO371.51001.9763. Nov. 25, 1945.

Bird Library, Syracuse University. Francis Biddle Papers.

Dostert, Léon. "The Instantaneous Multi-Lingual Interpreting System in the International Military Tribunal." Ts. Box 15.

Egbert, Lawrence D., Haakon M. Chevalier, and C.D. MacIntosh. "Glossary of Legal Terms French-English." Ts. Box 15.

International Military Tribunal. Seventeenth Organizational Meeting. Oct. 29, 1945, 10:10 a.m. Ts. Box 1. Minutes.

———. Eighteenth Organizational Meeting. Oct. 29, 1945, 2:20 p.m. Ts. Box 1. Minutes.

———. Notes of Evidence. Nov. 20, 1945. Ts. 1: 9. Box 3.

———. Notes of Evidence. Nov. 22, 1945. Ts. 1: 23. Box 3.

———. Executive Session. Nov. 24, 1945. Ts. Box 2.

———. Notes of Evidence. Nov. 26, 1945. Ts. 1: 40, 43. Box 3.

———. Executive Session. Nov. 28, 1945. Ts. Box 2.

———. Notes of Evidence. Dec. 12, 1945. Ts. 1: 147. Box 3.

Other Unpublished Material

AIIC, "Vertrag und Allgemeine Vertragsbedingungen für Konferenzdolmetscher."

"Current Translating Division Personnel List." Ts. Spring 1946.

Holt, A.C. "International Understanding: A Tribute to Mr. Thomas J. Watson." Ts. IBM Archives, Somers.

"IBM Wireless Translating System Embodying the Filene-Finlay Patents." Ts. New York, September 1947. IBM Archives, Somers.

"Information Concerning Interpreters." Ts. Spring 1946.

International Military Tribunal. Personnel Index Cards. Ms. and ts. Nuremberg, 1945-1946.

Keating, Kathleen. "The Role of the Interpreter in the Trial Process."

Office of Chief of Counsel for War Crimes. Letter of Commendation to E.P. Uiberall. Ts. Aug. 4, 1948.

Steer, Alfred Gilbert, Jr. "Translating Division." Ts. July 15, 1946.

——. "Participation of Allied Delegations in the Work of the Translating Division." Ts. July 30, 1946.

——. "Simultaneous Multi-Lingual Interpreting System." Ts. n.d.

——. "Interesting Times: Memoir of Service in U.S. Navy, 1941-1947." Ts. 1992.

Uiberall, Ernest Peter. "Court Interpreting at the Nuremberg Trial." Ts. April 11, 1995.

——. "Simultaneous Interpreters at the Nuremberg Trials." Ts. July 25, 1995.

United Nations Secretariat News. "George Khlebnikov (1923-1996), brought rapid-fire linguistic skills from the Nuremberg trials to the first United Nations Assembly." Ts. n.d. Obituary.

Personal Correspondence

AIIC. Letter to the author. Feb. 17, 1995.

Coliver, Edith S. Letter to the author. April 17, 1995.

——. Letter to the author. Aug. 2, 1995.

Heyward, Elisabeth. Letter to the author. April 14, 1995.

——. Letter to the author. May 1, 1995.

——. Letter to the author. Mar. 3, 1997.

——. Letter to the author. May 20, 1997.

Horn, Nancy. Letter to the author. March 1997.

Horn, Stefan F. Letter to the author. Aug. 27, 1995.

Horsky, Charles A. Letter to the author. April 21, 1995.

——. Letter to the author. April 27, 1995.

Jordan, Patricia. Letter to the author. Mar. 14, 1997.

Ramler, Siegfried. Curriculum vitae.

——. Letter to the author. Feb. 1, 1995.

——. Letter to the author. Feb. 13, 1995.

——. Letter to the author. Mar. 11, 1997.

Skuncke, Marie-France. Letter to the author. April 4, 1997.

Sprecher, Drexel A. Letter to the author. Mar. 4, 1997.

Steer, Alfred Gilbert, Jr. Curriculum vitae. 1980.

——. Letter to the author. Jan. 21, 1995.

——. Letter to the author. Feb. 14, 1995.

——. Letter to the author. April 7, 1995.

——. Letter to the author. April 22, 1995.

——. Letter to the author. Sept. 7, 1995.

——. Letter to the author. April 15, 1996.

——. Letter to the author. Feb. 11, 1997.

——. Letter to the author. March 1997.

Treidell, Frederick C. Letter to the author. Aug. 29, 1995.

Uiberall, Ernest Peter. Letter to the author. Feb. 11, 1995.

——. Letter to the author. Feb. 25, 1995.

——. Letter to the author. April 10, 1995.

——. Letter to the author. April 27, 1995.

——. Letter to the author. July 8, 1995.

——. Letter to the author. July 26, 1995.

——. Letter to the author. May 21, 1996.

——. Letter to the author. Feb. 3, 1997.

——. Letter to the author. Feb. 3, 1997.

——. Telephone Interview. Jan. 26, 1995.

Microfilms, Audio- and Videorecording

AIIC. *Nurnberg.* Videocassette. Geneva, 1992.

AIIC. *The Interpreters: A Historical Perspective.* Videocassette, 51 minutes. AIIC Conference. Aug. 28-30, 1992. AIIC, *Nurnberg.*

Excerpts of the Original Videorecording of the Nuremberg Trial. AIIC, *Nurnberg.*

Göring, Hermann. Photo-Archiv Generalfeldmarschall Göring. Seven microfilm reels. Washington, D.C.: Library of Congress, Photoduplication Service, 1982.

Heyward, Elisabeth, and George (Youri) Khlebnikov. Interview. AIIC Videocassette.

Judgment at Nuremberg. Two videocassettes. Prod. by Stanley Kramer Production. Dir. by Stanley Kramer. Culver City: Roxlom Films, 1961. Starring S. Tracy, B. Lancaster, R. Widmark and M. Dietrich. Based on the homonymous play by Abby Mann. 190 min. b/w.

News of the Day. Videocassette with newsreel segments. Vol. 17, No. 227. Nov. 23, 1945. Excerpt. Latest films on Nuremberg Trial drama. Film and Television Archive, University of California Los Angeles.

News of the Day. Videocassette with newsreel segments. Vol. 18, No. 204. Sept. 16, 1946. Excerpts of the Nuremberg criminals' final pleas. Film and Television Archive, University of California Los Angeles.

News of the Day. Videocassette with newsreel segments. Vol. 18, No. 210. Sept. 16, 1946. Excerpts from the judgement day for Nazi gang at Nuremberg. Film and Television Archive, University of California Los Angeles.

Nine Men in Hell: True and Authentic Presentation of the Nuremberg Trials. Two film reels. Prod. Thunderbird Films, Los Angeles. 50 min. English version of the original Russian production.

Nuremberg. Two videocassettes. Washington, D.C.: National Audiovisual Center, War Department, 1946. 76 min.

Official Film of the Trial. Imperial War Museum, London.

Official Sound Recording of the Proceedings. National Archives, Washington, D.C.

Uiberall, Peter Ernest, and Rozalinda Meza-Steel. Interview. Videocassette. Hollin Hills, Aug. 22, 1992.

Books and Articles about the Nuremberg Trial

Alexander, Charles W. *Nürnberg.* Nürnberg: Ulrich, 1946.

———. *Justice at Nuremberg: A Pictorial Record of the Trial of Nazi War Criminals by the International Military Tribunal at Nuremberg.* Chicago: Marvel, 1946. Text by Anne Keeshan.

Andrus, Burton C. *The Infamous of Nuremberg.* London: Frewin, 1969. Rpt. as *I was the Nuremberg Jailer.* New York: Coward-McCann, 1969.

Appleman, John A. *Military Tribunals and International Crimes.* Indianapolis: Bobbs, 1954.

Baird, Jay W., ed. *From Nuremberg to My Lay.* Lexington: Heath, 1972.

Bardèche, Maurice. *Nuremberg ou la terre promise.* Paris: Les Sept Couleurs, 1948.

———. *Nuremberg II ou les faux monnayeurs.* Paris: Les Sept Couleurs, 1950.

Bardens, Dennis. *Lord Justice Birkett.* London: Hale, 1962.

Belgion, Montgomery. *Epitaph on Nuremberg: A Letter Intended to Have Been Sent to a Friend Temporarily Abroad.* London: Falcon, 1946.

———. *Victor's Justice: A Letter Intended to Have Been Sent to a Friend Recently in Germany.* Hinsdale: Regnery, 1949.

Benton, Wilbourn E., ed. *Nuremberg: German Views of the War Trials.* Dallas: Southern Methodist University Press, 1955.

Bernstein, Victor H. *Final Judgement: The Story of Nuremberg.* New York: Boni, 1947.

Biddle, Francis. *In Brief Authority.* Garden City: Doubleday, 1962.

Bosch, William J. *Judgement on Nuremberg: American Attitudes toward the Major German War-Crimes Trials.* Chapel Hill: University of North Carolina Press, 1970.

"British Case at Nuremberg." *The Times,* Dec. 3, 1945: 4.

"British Evidence at Nuremberg." *The Times*, Nov. 29, 1945: 4.

Bross, Werner. *Gespräche mit Hermann Göring während der Nürnberger Prozesse*. Flensburg: Wolff, 1950.

Calvocoressi, Peter. *Nuremberg: The Facts, the Law and the Consequences*. London: Chatto, 1947.

"Captured Documents." *The Times*, Nov. 23, 1945: 4.

CBS News. *Trial at Nuremberg*. By the staff of CBS News. Project ed. by William Saphiro. New York: Watts, 1967.

"The Chalice of Nürnberg." *Time*, Dec. 10, 1945: 26.

Conot, Robert E. *Justice at Nuremberg*. New York: Harper, 1983.

Cooper, Robert W. *The Nuremberg Trial*. Harmondsworth: Penguin, 1947.

Davidson, Eugene. *The Trial of the Germans: An Account of the Twenty-Two Defendants before the International Military Tribunal at Nuremberg*. New York: Macmillan, 1966.

Dos Passos, John. "Report from Nürnberg." *Life*, Dec. 10, 1945: 29-30. Also in Baird.

Fritzsche, Hans. *Hier spricht Hans Fritzsche*. Zurich: Interverlag 1948. Rpt. as *Es sprach Hans Fritzsche: nach den Gesprächen, Briefen und Dokumenten*. Ed. by Hildegard Springer. Stuttgart: Thiele, 1949.

——. *The Sword in the Scales: As Told to Hildegard Springer*. Trans. by D. Pyke and H. Fraenkel. London: Wingate, 1953. Trans. of *Das Schwert auf der Waage*. Heidelberg: Vowinckel, 1953.

Gaskin, Hilary, ed. *Eyewitnesses at Nuremberg*. London: Arms, 1990.

Gerhart, Eugene C. *America's Advocate: Robert H. Jackson*. Indianapolis: Bobbs, 1958.

"Germany: The Defendants." *Time*, Oct. 29, 1945: 38.

"Germany: Interpreters and Mistresses." *The Time*, Oct. 15, 1945: 30.

Gilbert, Gustave M. *Nuremberg Diary*. New York: Farrar, 1947. Trans. of *Nürnberger Tagebuch 1947*. Frankfurt am Mein: Fischer, 1947.

Glueck, Sheldon. *War Criminals: Their Prosecution and Punishment*. New York: Knopf, 1944.

Göring, Hermann. *Le Procès de Nuremberg*. Paris: Office Français d'Édition, Service d'Information des Crimes de Guerre, 1946-.

——. *Highlights from the Direct and Cross-Examination of Hermann Göring in the Nuremberg Trial*. Minnetonka: Professional Education Group, 1988.

"Great Nuremberg Trial Opens." *The Times*, Nov. 21, 1945: 4.

Grun, Bernard, ed. *The Timetables of History*. New York: Simon and Schuster, 1975.

Gründler, Gerhard E., and Arnim von Manikowsky. *Nuremberg ou la justice des vainqueurs*. Trans. by Herbert Lugert. Paris: Laffont, 1969. Trans. of *Das Gericht der Sieger: der Prozeß gegen Hess, Ribbentrop, Keitel, Kaltenbrunner u.a.* Oldenburg: Stalling, 1967.

Haensel, Carl. *Das Gericht vertagt sich: aus dem Tagebuch eines Nürnberger Verteidigers.* Hamburg: Classen, 1950.

Harris, Whitney R. *Tyranny on Trial: The Evidence at Nuremberg.* Dallas: Southern Methodist Press, 1954.

Harwood, Richard E. *Nuremberg and Other War Crimes Trials: A New Look.* Southam: Historical Review Press, 1978.

Hauser, Ernest O. "The Backstage Battle at Nuremberg." *Saturday Evening Post* [Philadelphia], Jan. 19, 1946: 18+.

Heydecker, Joe J. *The Nuremberg Trial: A History of Nazi Germany as Revealed through the Testimony at Nuremberg.* Trans. and ed. by R.A. Downie. London: Heinemann, 1962. Trans. of *Der Nürnberger Prozeß.* Köln: Kiepenheuer, 1950.

———. *Bilanz der Tausend Jahre: die Geschichte des Dritten Reiches im Spiegel der Nürnberger Prozesse.* München: Heyne, 1975.

———, and Johannes Leeb. *Der Nürnberger Prozeß: Neue Dokumente, Erkenntnisse und Analysen.* Köln: Kiepenheuer, 1979.

Hyde, Montgomery H. *Lord Justice: The Life and Times of Lord Birkett of Ulverston.* New York: Random, 1964.

International Military Tribunal. *Anklageschrift des Internationalen Militärgerichtshofes gegen die 24 Nazistischen Kriegsverbrecher.* Germany: Militärgerichtshof?, 1945?

———. *The Trial of German Major War Criminals: Proceedings of the International Military Tribunal Sitting at Nuremberg, Germany, 20th November, 1945 to (1st October, 1946).* London: Stationery Office, 1946-(1951).

———. *Nürnberger Urteil.* Düsseldorf: Schwann, 1946.

———. *Das Urteil von Nürnberg: vollständiger Text.* München: Nymphenburger, 1946.

———. *Trial of the Major War Criminals before the International Military Tribunal, Nuremberg, 14 November 1945—1 October 1946.* 42 vols. Blue Series. Nuremberg, 1947.

———. *Der Prozeß Gegen die Hauptkriegsverbrecher vor dem Internationalen Militärgerichtshof, Nürnberg, 14. November 1945—1. Oktober 1946.* Nürnberg, 1947-.

Jackson, Robert H. *The Case against the Nazi War Criminals: Opening Statement for the United States of America by Robert H. Jackson and Other Documents.* New York: Knopf, 1946.

———. *Report of Robert H. Jackson, United States Representative, to the International Conference on Military Trial, London, 1945.* Department of State publication 3080. Division of Publications. Office of Public Affairs, February 1949.

Kahn, Leo. *Nuremberg Trials.* New York: Ballantine, 1972.

Kilmuir, David Maxwell-Fyfe. *Nuremberg in Retrospect.* Birmingham: The Holdsworth Club of the University of Birmingham, 1956.

———. *Political Adventure: The Memoirs of the Earl of Kilmuir.* London: Weidenfeld, 1964.

Knieriem, August von. *The Nuremberg Trials.* Chicago: Regnery, 1959.

Lazard, Didier. *Le procès de Nuremberg: récit d'un témoin.* Paris: Éditions de la Nouvelle France, 1947.

Lebedeva, Nataliia. "The USSR and the Nuremberg Trial." *International Affairs* 42.5-6 (1996): 233-254.

Lessing, Holger. *Der Erste Dachauer Prozess (1945/46).* Baden-Baden: Nomos, 1993.

Lewis, John R. *Uncertain Judgement: A Bibliography of War Crimes Trials.* Santa Barbara: ABC-Clio, 1979.

Lippe, Viktor, Freiherr von der. *Nürnberger Tagebuchnotizien: November 1945 bis Oktober 1946.* Frankfurt am Mein: Knapp, 1951.

McMillan, James. *Five Men at Nuremberg.* London: Harrap, 1985.

Mann, Abby. *Judgement at Nuremberg.* New York: New American Library, 1961.

Maser, Werner. *Nuremberg: A Nation on Trial.* Trans. by Richard Barry. New York: Scribner, 1979. Trans. of *Nürnberg, Tribunal der Sieger.* Düsseldorf: Econ, 1977.

———. *Das Exempel: Der Nürnberger Prozeß als historisches Problem; zwei Vorlesungen.* Asendorf: Mut, 1986.

Merle, Marcel. *Le procès de Nuremberg et le châtiment des criminels de guerre.* Paris: Pedone, 1949.

Neave, Airey. *Nuremberg: A Personal Record of the Trial of the Major Nazi Criminals in 1945-46.* London: Cornet, 1978.

———. *On Trial at Nuremberg.* Boston: Little, 1978.

"News Reels: The Nuremberg Trial." *The Times,* Nov. 30, 1945: 6.

O'Barr, William M. *Linguistic Evidence: Language Power and Strategies in the Courtroom.* New York: Academic, 1982.

Office of the United States Chief of Counsel for the Prosecution of Axis Criminality. *Nazi Conspiracy and Aggression.* 8 vols. Washington, D.C.: Government Printing Office, 1946.

———. *Nazi Conspiracy and Aggression.* Supplement A: Prosecution. Supplement B: Defense and Interrogations. Washington, D.C.: Government Printing Office, 1948.

Persico, Joseph E. *Nuremberg: Infamy on Trial.* New York: Viking-Penguin, 1994.

Poltorak, Arkadii Iosifovich. *Nürnberger Epilog.* Berlin: Militärverlag der DDR, 1971. Trans. of *Niurnbergskii Epilog.* Moskva: Voenizsdat, 1969.

———, and Y. Zaitsev. *Remember Nuremberg.* Moscow: Foreign Language Publishing, 1961.

"Rapid Procedure at Nuremberg." *The Times,* Oct. 30, 1945: 3.

"Rehearsal is Held for Crimes Trials." *The New York Times*, Nov. 6, 1945: 14.

Robinson, Jacob, and Henry Sachs. *The Holocaust: The Nuremberg Evidence.* Part I: Documents. Jerusalem: Yad Vashem, 1976.

Röling, B.V.A. *The Tokyo Trial and Beyond: Reflections of a Peacemonger.* Cambridge: Polity, 1993.

"Russians Delay War Crimes Study." *The New York Times*, Oct. 15, 1945: 6.

Saurel, Louis. *Le Procès de Nuremberg.* Paris: Rouff, 1967.

Schmidt, Dana A. "Pick Your Language." *The New York Times Magazine*, VI, Aug. 25, 1946: 24.

Schmidt, Paul Otto. *Hitler's Interpreter.* Ed. by R.H.C. Steed. London: Heinemann, 1950.

Schneider, Rolf. *Prozeß in Nürnberg.* Frankfurt am Mein: Fischer, 1968.

Sheean, Vincent. "Error in Translation: Nuremberg and Menschlichkeit." *United Nations World* I (September 1947): 28-29.

Smith, Bradley F. *Reaching Judgement at Nuremberg.* New York: Basic, 1977.

——. *The Road to Nuremberg.* New York: Basic, 1981.

——, ed. *The American Road to Nuremberg: The Documentary Record 1944-1945.* Stanford: Hoover Institution, 1982.

——. *Der Jahrhundert Prozeß: die Motive der Richter von Nürnberg; Anatomie einer Urteilsfindung.* Trans. from English by Günther Danehl. Frankfurt am Mein: Fischer, 1983.

Speer, Albert. *Inside the Third Reich: Memoirs by Albert Speer.* Trans. by Richard and Clara Winston. London: Macmillan, 1970.

Steiniger, P.A., ed. *Der Nürnberger Prozeß: aus den Protokollen, Dokumenten und Materialien des Prozesses gegen die Hauptkriegsverbrecher vor dem Internationalen Militärgerichthof.* 2 vols. Berlin: Rütten, 1951.

Sulzberger, C.L. "Jackson Stresses Allies' Trial Unity." *The New York Times*, Mar. 10, 1946: 5.

Taylor, Telford. *Final Report to the Secretary of the Army on the Nurnberg War Crimes Trials under Control Council Law No. 10.* Washington, D.C.: Government Printing Office, 1949.

——. *Nuremberg Trials: War Crimes and International Law.* New York: Carnegie Endowment for International Peace, 1949.

——. *Die Nürnberger Prozesse: Kriegsverbrechen und Völkerrecht.* Trans. by Ruth Kempner. Zürich: Europa Verlag, 1951. Trans. of *Nuremberg Trials: War Crimes and International Law.*

——. *Nürnberg and Vietnam: An American Tragedy.* Chicago: Quadrangle, 1970.

——. *The Anatomy of the Nuremberg Trials: A Personal Memoir.* New York: Knopf, 1992.

"Trials of War Criminals." *The Times,* Oct. 17, 1945: 2.

Truman, Harry S. Executive Order 9547. *Code of Federal Regulations.* Title 3, suppl. 2, 1943-1948. Washington, D.C.: United States Government Printing Office, 1951.

———. Executive Order 9626. *Code of Federal Regulations.* Title 3, suppl. 2, 1943-1948. Washington, D.C.: United States Government Printing Office, 1951.

———. Executive Order 9679. *Code of Federal Regulations.* Title 3, suppl. 2, 1943-1948. Washington, D.C.: United States Government Printing Office, 1951.

Tusa, Ann, and John Tusa. *The Nuremberg Trial.* London: Macmillan, 1983.

United Nations General Assembly. International Law Commission. *The Charter and Judgement of the Nürnberg Trial: History and Analysis.* Memorandum submitted by the Secretary General. Lake Success: United Nations, 1949.

United States. Department of State. *Trial of War Criminals.* Documents: 1. Report of Robert H. Jackson to the President. 2. Agreement establishing an International Military Tribunal. 3. Indictment. Washington, D.C.: Government Printing Office, 1945.

"War Crimes." *Encyclopaedia Britannica.*

"War Crimes." *Encyclopedia Americana.*

"War Crimes." *Time,* Oct. 26, 1945: 28.

Wellman, Francis. *The Art of Cross-Examination: With the Cross-Examination of Important Witnesses in Some Celebrated Cases.* 1903. 4th ed., rev. and enl. New York: Collier-Macmillan, 1936.

Werner, Karl Heinz, ed. *Nürnberger Prozeß, gestern und heute.* Berlin: Staatsverlag der DDR, 1966.

West, Rebecca D. *A Train of Powder.* New York: Viking, 1955.

Wieland, Günther. *Der Jahrhundertprozeß von Nürnberg: Nazi- und Kriegsverbrecher vor Gericht.* Berlin: Staatsverlag der DDR, 1986.

Wilkins, William. *The Sword and the Gavel: An Autobiography.* Seattle: Writing Works, 1981.

Winward, Walter. *The Canaris Fragment.* New York: Morrow, 1983.

Books and Articles about Interpreting

American Translators Association. *ATA Professional Services Directory.* Croton-on-Hudson: ATA, 1965-1969, 1976.

———. *Membership List of ATA.* Croton-on-Hudson: ATA, 1965, 1969, 1978, 1979, 1980, 1982, 1983, 1985, 1986, 1987.

———. "Court Interpreting and the Testing and Licensing of Interpreters." *ATA Chronicle* Oct.-Nov. (1979): 6-7.

———. *Silver Tongues.* Proceedings of the 25th annual conference of ATA. Ed. by Patricia E. Newman. Medford: Learned Information, 1984.

——. *Translation Services Directory 1983-*. Medford: ATA, 1986.

——. *Building Bridges*. Proceedings of the 27th annual conference of ATA. Ed. by Karl Kummer. Medford: Learned Information, 1986.

——. *Across the Language Gap*. Proceedings of the 28th annual conference of ATA. Ed. by Karl Kummer. Medford: Learned Information, 1987.

——. *Languages at Crossroads*. Proceedings of the 29th annual conference of ATA. Ed. by Deanna Lindberg Hammond. Medford: Learned Information, 1988.

——. *Coming of Age*. Proceedings of the 30th annual conference of ATA. Ed. by Deanna Lindberg Hammond. Medford: Learned Information, 1989.

——. *Interpreting: Yesterday, Today, and Tomorrow*. Ed. by David and Margareta Bowen. American Translators Association Scholarly Monograph Series IV. Binghamton: State University of New York at Binghamton, 1990.

——. *Looking Ahead: ATA in '92*. Proceedings of the 31st annual conference of ATA. Ed. Amos Leslie Willson. Medford: Learned Information, 1990.

Austin, William M., ed. *Papers in Linguistics in Honor of Léon Dostert*. The Hague: Mouton, 1967.

Bohlen, Charles E. *Witnesses to History: 1929-1969*. New York: Norton, 1973.

Bourgain, Gilbert. "A Genève, retour de Nuremberg." *AIIC Bulletin* 19.4 (1991): 18-19.

Bowen, David, and Margareta Bowen. "The Nuremberg Trials: Communication through Translation." *Meta* [Montreal] 30.1 (1985): 74-77.

——. "Editors' Remarks." ATA, *Interpreting: Yesterday* 1-7.

Bower, William W. *International Manual of Linguists and Translators*. New York: Scarecrow, 1959.

——. *International Manual of Linguists and Translators*. Supplement. New York: Scarecrow, 1961.

Chernov, Gelij V. "Conference Interpretation in the U.S.S.R.: History, Theory, New Frontiers." *Meta* 37.1 (1992): 149-162.

Chevalier, Haakon M. *Oppenheimer: The Story of a Friendship*. New York: Braziller, 1965.

Congrat-Butlar, Stefan. *Translation and Translators: An International Directory and Guide*. New York: Bowker, 1979.

Dollman, Eugen. *The Interpreter: Memoirs*. Trans. by J. Maxwell Brownjohn. London: Hutchinson, 1967. Trans. of *Dolmetscher der Diktatoren*.

"École d'Interprètes de l'Université de Genève." *L'Interprète* 2 (1952).

"École d'Interprètes." *L'Interprète* 4 (1952): 10.

Fuchs-Vidotto, Letizia B. "Zum erstenmal Simultananlage vor Gericht." *Babel* [Budapest] 3 (1982): 162.

Gerver, D., and Wallace H. Sinaiko, eds. *Language Interpretation and Communication*. Proceedings of the NATO Symposium on Language Interpretation and Communication. New York: Plenum, 1978.

Gile, Daniel. "Bibliographie de l'Interprétation auprès des Tribunaux." *Parallelès* 11 (1989): 105-112.

Harris, Brian. "Observations on a Cause Célèbre: Court Interpreting at the Lischka Trial." Roberts 189-201.

Herbert, Jean. "How Conference Interpretation Grew." Gerver 5-10.

Kaminker, André. "Conférence prononcée à l'Université de Genève." *L'Interprète* 10.3 (1955): 9-12.

Kaminker, André. "Conférence prononcée à l'Université de Genève (Part Two)." *L'Interprète* 10.4 (1955): 9-12.

Koch, Andreas. "Übersetzen und Dolmetschen im Ersten Nürnberger Kriegsverbrecherprozeß." *Lebende Sprachen* 37.1 (1992): 1-7.

Kelly, Louis G. *The True Interpreter: A History of the Translation Theory and Practice in the West.* Oxford: Blackwell, 1979.

"Language Barriers Broken by I.B.M. Simultaneous Interpretation System." *Audio Record*, December 1951.

Lederer, Marianne. *La traduction simultanée: expérience et théorie.* Paris: Lettres Modernes, 1981.

"Leon Dostert, 67, Dies: Expert on Languages." *Star*, Sept. 3, 1971.

Lévy-Berlowitz, Ruth. "The Linguistic Logistics of the Demjanjuk Trial." *Parallèles* 11 (1989): 37-44.

"Linguist Leon Dostert, GU Language Director." *Washington Post*, Sept. 3, 1971.

MacDonald, Ross R. "Léon Dostert." Austin 9-14.

Morris, Philip, and Geoff Weston, eds. *Directory of Translators and Translating Agencies in the UK.* London: Bowker-Saur, 1987. 2nd ed. 1990.

Morris, Ruth. "Eichmann vs. Demjanjuk: A Study of Interpreted Proceedings." *Parallèles* 11 (1989): 9-28.

——. "The Impact of Interpretation at Legal Proceedings on Participants' Role Performance." M.A. thesis. Communication Institute, Hebrew University, Jerusalem, 1989.

——. "Technology and the Worlds of Interpreting." In *Future and Communication: The Role of Scientific and Technical Communication and Translation in Technology Development and Transfer.* International Scholars Publications. Ed. by Y. Gitay and D. Porush. San Francisco: Rousenhouse, 1997. 177-184.

Northern California Translators Association. *Professional Directory 1983-84.* San Francisco: NCTA, 1984.

Obst, Harry, and Ruth H. Cline. "Summary History of Language Services." ATA, *Interpreting: Yesterday* 8-13.

Philadelphia Guild of Professional Translators. *Translator Referral Directory.* Philadelphia: PGPT, 1977.

Ramler, Siegfried. "Origins and Challenges of Simultaneous Interpretation: The Nuremberg Trial Experience." ATA, *Languages at Crossroads* 437-440.

"Résultats des examens pour l'obtention du diplôme." *L'Interprète*, October 1951: 19; March 1952: 13; July 1952: 11.

Roberts, Roda P., ed. *L'interprétation auprès des tribunaux.* Proceedings of the meeting held on April 10 and 11, 1980 at the University of Ottawa. Ottawa: University of Ottawa Press, 1981.

Roditi, Edouard. "The History of Interpretation in a Nutshell." (1982) National Resource Center for Translation and Interpreting, Georgetown University, Washington, D.C. Rpt. as "Interpreting: Its History in a Nutshell." N.d. National Resource Center for Translation and Interpreting, Georgetown University, Washington, D.C.

Schuker, Theodore. "The Amoco Cadiz Case." *Parallèles* 11 (1989): 75-92.

Skinner, William, and Thomas F. Carson. "Working Conditions at the Nuremberg Trials." Interview. ATA, *Interpreting: Yesterday* 14-22.

Skuncke, Marie-France. "Tout a commencé à Nuremberg." *Parallèles* 11 (1989): 5-8.

"Steer, Alfred Gilbert, Jr." *Who's Who in America.* Chicago: Marquis Who's Who, 1983 and 1991.

Tayler, Marilyn R. *Skills for Bilingual Legal Personnel.* Glenview: Scott, 1985.

"Telephonic Interpretation—The System of the Future?" *L'Interprète* 1.5 (August/September 1946): 2-4.

Université de Genève. "Conference Interpretation at the École de Traduction et d'Interprétation." Leaflet.

Van Hoof, Henri. *Théorie et pratique de l'interprétation: avec application particulière à l'anglais et au français.* Munich: Max Hueber Verlag, 1962.

Wilss, Wolfram. "Syntactic Anticipation in German-English Simultaneous Interpreting." Gerver 343-352.

INDEX